RAINCOAST CHRONICLES

-19-

Stories and History of the British Columbia Coast

Edited by
HOWARD WHITE

HARBOUR PUBLISHING

Copyright © 2003 Harbour Publishing

All rights reserved. No part of this publication may be reproduced, stored in a retrieval system or transmitted, in any form or by any means, without prior permission of the publisher or, in the case of photocopying or other reprographic copying, a licence from Access Copyright, the Canadian Copyright Licensing Agency, 1 Yonge Street, Suite 1900, Toronto, Ontario, M5E 1E5, www.accesscopyright.ca, 1-800-893-5777, info@accesscopyright.ca.

Published by
Harbour Publishing Co. Ltd., P.O. Box 219, Madeira Park, BC V0N 2H0
www.harbourpublishing.com

Cover design by Charon O'Brien
Page design by Martin Nichols
Cover artwork by Bill Maximick
Printed and bound in Canada

Harbour Publishing acknowledges financial support from the Government of Canada through the Book Publishing Industry Development Program and the Canada Council for the Arts; and from the Province of British Columbia through the British Columbia Arts Council and the Book Publisher's Tax Credit through the Ministry of Provincial Revenue.

National Library of Canada Cataloguing in Publication Data

Main entry under title:
Raincoast chronicles 19/edited by Howard White.

ISBN 1-55017-316-2

1. Pacific Coast (B.C.)—History. I. White, Howard, 1945– II. Title: Raincoast chronicles nineteen.
FC3803.R349 2003 971.1'1 C2003-910651-9 F1086.R349 2003

TABLE *of* CONTENTS

Without Deed or Permit

Squatters in the Lower Mainland

Sheryl Salloum

On September 14, 2002, a group of homeless people and housing activists occupied the old Woodward's building on Hastings Street in Vancouver, empty and unused since the department store went bankrupt in 1993. They were angered by the failure of repeated attempts to broker a deal that would convert some or all of the block-sized structure to social housing.

A week later police evicted about 25 occupants, but soon afterward a throng of squatters erected a community of sorts on the sidewalk surrounding the building. For three months the "Woodward's Squat," as it came to be known, focussed the entire city's attention on issues of social housing, homelessness and the general neglect of Vancouver's Downtown Eastside.

At its peak the squat was home to an estimated 280 people, but their numbers had dwindled to about 100 by December 14, when a new, left-leaning city council, with federal help, arranged temporary quarters for 54 of the squatters and promised to find a more permanent solution to the inner city's housing crisis.

As squatters' settlements go, the Woodward's Squat was more of a political statement than a

Tim Cummings, the last sanctioned squatter in Stanley Park, chops firewood outside his Brockton Point shack. Born in the area in 1881 to one of the original squatter families, Cummings snubbed negotiations to relocate squatters, noting that no one consulted his family before it became a park. He stayed put until his death in 1958. *Photo courtesy Vancouver Public Library*

The squatters' community on Deadman's Island in Stanley Park, seen around 1898-1900, when it was more than a decade old. Most of the homes were built on logs, floating at high tide, resting on the beach at low tide. Their occupants fished in the harbour for a living; some grew vegetables and even raised livestock. *Photo courtesy City of Vancouver Archives*

serious attempt at homesteading, but it takes its place in the rich, varied and almost unbroken tradition of squatting in the Lower Mainland over the last 140 years. In the words of Malcolm Lowry, perhaps the region's most famous squatter, the homes of squatters "with their weathered sidings [are] as much a part of the natural surrounding as a Shinto temple is of the Japanese landscape."

Squatters' communities have evolved in Greater Vancouver for various reasons, including poverty, rebellion against social conventions and the yearning for a way of life that harmonizes with natural surroundings. A temperate climate and the ready availability of unused property, water, food and fuel have made settlement feasible for even the poorest residents. Local waterways provided fish for eating and selling; driftwood could be gathered for home heating and cooking; boats provided transportation. While many of the settlements were established in isolated areas, they were close enough to Vancouver and its satellite municipalities that service industries were always nearby.

The history of squatters in Vancouver goes back at least as far as 1860, when Portuguese and Scottish sailors jumped ship in Vancouver's harbour and settled in what is now Stanley Park. The land was an ancestral burial and fishing ground for the Coast Salish Indians, heavily forested and inhabited by bears and cougars. The sailors married aboriginal women and built one-storey homes of axe-hewn lumber near the sandy beach at Brockton Point. At that time, the harbour was teeming with herring and the sailors made a living fishing the abundant waters. The squatters supplemented their food supply by planting gardens and raising chickens and other livestock. Their community was known locally as Fishermen's Cove, Fishermen's Village, Squatters' Village or Indian Portage.

In 1888, the year that Stanley Park officially opened, a smallpox epidemic swept through Vancouver. The health inspector had the squatters' houses razed; compensation was $150. The families rebuilt, but their tenancy became more difficult. A roadway was built around the park and more people used the lands more often. Inevitably, those who saw the houses as eyesores and those who were interested in developing the area commercially applied pressure to have the squatters evicted. Their lobby was not successful until 1921, when the city began legal eviction proceedings against the park's inhabitants: nine descendants of the original Stanley Park squatters.

To establish squatters' rights, the residents had to prove 60 years of continuous occupancy, a difficult task without deeds or other written documentation. Tom Abraham, a Native thought to be 110 years old at the time, testified that he "had made no record like the white man, but remembered by events, such as the Cariboo gold rush." Abraham recalled that at that time (1859–1865) there were "four buildings on land now occupied by the squatters." But an 1863 map prepared by Corporal George Turner of the Royal Engineers did not show the homes of the defendants, and Mr. Justice Murphy declared the

On the north shore of False Creek in 1934, a squatter saws driftwood for his stove aboard one of the boats and float homes moored near the CPR roundhouse. Railway workers, First World War veterans, families and hoboes coexisted peacefully in squatter communities on both sides of False Creek during the Depression. Although civic authorities grumbled about the 'eyesores,' they seldom enforced eviction notices, preferring not to add to the relief rolls.
Photo courtesy City of Vancouver Archives

evidence of all but one squatter inconclusive and "unsatisfactory." Mariah Kulkalem was the only one who managed to prove 60 years of uninterrupted residency. The others appealed their cases, but lost in 1925. They were allowed to remain in their homes for one dollar a month until they were evicted in 1931, their homes and outbuildings burned by the Vancouver Fire Department.

Tim Cummings, who was born in 1881 and whose family had been among the first squatters, did not participate in the court battle. He felt that since his family had not been consulted when the land they inhabited was turned into a park, he did not have to comply with eviction orders. Instead, Cummings came to an "understanding" with the parks board, and he and his sister Agnes were granted continued tenancy for the sum of $5 a month. Both lived in Stanley Park until their deaths, Agnes in 1953 at the age of 69 and Tim in 1958 at the age of 77.

Some time after the squatter community at Brockton Point was built, another illegal village took shape on the small finger of land south of the park—Deadman's Island. Most of the homes there were built atop logs on the foreshore; at high tide they would float and at low tide they would rest on the shoreline. In 1909, all of the squatters, numbering close to 150, were evicted. They soon returned and on April 30, 1912, their shacks were raided. "Men from the sheriff's office carried the firebrand... and burned to the ground" about 40 dwellings. In 1924, squatters again began settling on the island. Most were fishermen, some of whom had been evicted from Stanley Park. Many moored houseboats on the small island. They were evicted in 1930 but some people stayed on in their houseboats until the early 1940s.

Meanwhile, a number of other squatter communities were developing. In the November 7, 1936 issue of the *Daily Province*, Ogden H. Hershaw wrote that a community established in about 1900 was burgeoning beneath the Burrard Bridge, on the foreshore of the Kitsilano Reserve and should be "preserved." The tumbledown dwellings of "Bumtown" or "Bennettville" (a derisive reference to Depression-era Prime Minister R.B. Bennett) were home to some 300 proud but poor people, a city within a city. One man, a Swedish immigrant of 10 years, made his living by fishing, screening sand and salvaging logs. He proudly stressed,

> I have never been on relief, but should the government evacuate us... the majority of us will become a public liability... If they really wanted to help us, let them give us sewers and sidewalks, house numbers and the odd coat of paint. If, then, the Parks Board would give us some flower seed, we could work wonders around here.

Eviction notices were regularly given to the "Bumtown" residents, but neither the city of Vancouver, nor the province, nor the federal government seemed interested in enforcing the notices. In the *Daily Province*, Norman Hacking wrote that most residents attended to "their own business, sawing up wood for the winter, building additions to their homes, patching up tar paper, mending boats." They had been receiving eviction notices for at least nine years, and as one man explained, "They don't mean nothin'. Government's gotta get rid o' them notices, so they paste 'em up here." The squatters were right. No one was going to be dispossessed during the Dirty Thirties—Vancouver did not want to add to its relief rolls. New ramshackle dwellings appeared. Shantytowns developed on the banks of the Fraser River east of Nanaimo Street and stretched as far as New Westminster. Others were built on False Creek, along the northern and southern shores of Burrard Inlet, and in Richmond. Most of the communities lasted for decades.

The one exception was a "jungle" of unemployed and desperate men who congregated on property belonging to the Canadian Pacific Railway, east of Dunlevy Avenue, on the edge of Burrard Inlet.

Founded by Finnish immigrants in 1892, Finn Slough is the oldest squat in BC. Its modest floating homes have always been comfortable and well maintained, albeit Spartan—washing machines and refrigerators did not appear in the community until 1959. *Photo courtesy John Skapski*

During the 1930s, hundreds of destitute men rode freight trains into Vancouver in search of employment. Upon arriving, they found little work and took to squatting near the rail line. Col. R.D. Williams, the harbour commissioner, witnessed the formation of the squatters' "jungle." On a day of torrential spring rain in 1931, he saw "the legs of a man disappear under a pile of rails which lay on the CPR right of way... The rails were stacked four or five high... [and] the men had added some paper in sheets to add to the protection from the elements afforded by the rails." When he investigated, Col. Williams found 14 men huddled under the makeshift shelter "and two of them were without boots." He found out that some were veterans of the Great War, and he immediately tried to help by securing donations of food, clothing and cigarettes. However, their numbers continued to increase, and at the jungle's peak there were approximately 240 men living there. By the autumn of 1931, Col. Williams said, an outbreak of typhoid closed the encampment, and its "improvised... nondescript... [and] wonderfully unique architecture; old boards, sheet iron, packing cases, and whatnot went up in flames."

At their height, squatter communities in Vancouver were home to about 1,800. Taxpayers complained that the illegal residents had city benefits without having to pay taxes. In fact, most cabin dwellers had no running water or electricity, no sewage or garbage disposal. For the down-and-out there was simply no other place to go than the city's slum areas—not an appealing alternative for those with children.

The Biiroinens were one such family. Mr. Biiroinen, who had been a logger, fell ill and then suffered years of unemployment. By 1941, he and his family had lived in their shack for five years. Mrs. Biiroinen said that living in their waterfront shanty had been a "godsend," which allowed them to remain independent and off relief. A reporter from the *Daily Province* noted:

> [The Biiroinen] "cabin" is a far cry from a squalid room in a tenement... It's only three rooms—but they're three airy, sunny rooms, clean and scrubbed, attractive as ingenuity can make them on a small income. There are flower boxes by the window and a large well-fenced veranda where Roy [the baby] can play in the sunlight and breathe the fresh salt air, away from the smells of the city.

Members of the harbour squatters' community did enjoy running water for a time: it was piped in from a home on nearby Wall Street until a new owner moved in and refused to continue what he considered an illegal activity. When one of the squatters, Mrs. Eva Pick, asked the city to provide water, the city engineer answered with eviction notices. Mrs. Biiroinen commented that her family would likely have to move to an east end rooming house: "We can't pay a high rent... We'd like to stay here, even if we do have to carry our water." Another squatter, an elderly veteran of the Great War who existed on a small pension, lamented that if he moved into a rooming house he could not keep his only companion, a terrier.

The waterfront residents won a small reprieve when port manager K.J. Burns told an investigating committee that the squatters were "completely law-abiding." He was "amazed at the cleanliness" of their homes. Nevertheless, 40 of the shacks were removed. The Harbours Board and the Canadian Pacific Railway then agreed to consider leasing property to the cabin dwellers or giving them a temporary easement.

Laundry hangs on clotheslines among squatters' homes viewed from the Burrard Bridge in the late 1930s, the twilight of squatting in False Creek. Industry and a wartime expansion of RCAF activity on the Kitsilano side of the inlet would soon put teeth into the perennial eviction notices. *Photo courtesy City of Vancouver Archives*

In 1937, Vancouver City Council again wanted to eradicate the communities, which council members and others considered unsightly, but the Second World War and a severe housing shortage stopped them from taking action. By 1947, *Maclean's* magazine reported the councillors were again complaining, calling the squatters "water rats" and describing their villages with terms such as "eyesore . . . potential fire hazard . . . potential health hazard," pointing to improper sewage facilities (even though the city was dumping its sewage into the inlet). Inexplicably, to city authorities, the squatters and their children enjoyed extremely good health; some shacks did burn down, but other property was not destroyed.

Some Vancouverites prospered because of the squatters. In the colony at the foot of Cardero Street, known as "Shaughnessy Heights" (named after a prestigious Vancouver residential district), landowners put out wharves and collected moorage fees of 20 cents per foot per month for boats, and $10 a month for houseboats. Water and electricity usually cost more. Accommodation here was as swank as the name of the community implied. Mil Smith, a 61-year-old who worked part-time in a cannery, had an electric refrigerator, radio, and oil-burning stove. Some floating houses contained hot showers. A grey-haired grandmother named Elizabeth Sharp owned a 50-year-old missionary boat, the *Sal Lal*. She found her accommodation much less expensive and more cheerful than the rooms she had rented uptown for $55 a month. Another boat, the *Kia Ora*, was built as a ferry in 1913 and provided her owner with a beautiful home. The only drawback to "Shaughnessy Heights" was its smelly black mud, in which garbage such as mattresses, tin cans and broken glass was embedded.

Vastly different from "Shaughnessy Heights" was the cluster of cabins in the False Creek settlement. There, according to *Maclean's* in November 1947, "weather-beaten boards, broken shingles and rusted tin signs covered the shapeless houses, the whole conglomerate assembly vaguely joined together by a tangled line of floating walk and shaky handrail." Not all False Creek squatters were happy about their situation. One couple, Mr. and Mrs. Penny, lived there only because they were "not old enough for the old-age pension, and not rich enough to buy retirement on solid ground." They had the comparative luxury of electrical service from BC Electric, but had to haul water: there was "the paradox of people carrying fresh water 100 yards in pails to fill up their slick new washing machines."

Those on the Kitsilano Reserve side of False Creek had to contend with "a mixture of smells, all unpleasant." Life there was "primitive—no rent, no wharfage, no electricity, no running water." Similar settlements existed farther up Burrard Inlet: one on the south side stretched from the foot of Boundary Road to the Belcarra area of Burnaby; one on the north side had been built near Deep Cove, North Vancouver.

In September 1946, two young veterans of World War II and their families became squatters in another area of town. After 17 months of searching for a proper home for his wife and three-year-old son, John Robert Cox decided to move his family into the unused army huts at the Little Mountain Military camp near Heather and 41st Avenue in Vancouver. They were joined by another veteran, Bill Mooy, his wife and their 16-month-old son. Both men were from the Prairies and were given no priority for accommodation at a time of severe housing shortages.

The corporal guarding the gate was not prepared to deal with the arrival of two young women, their babies and their bedding. The *Daily Province* reported that the squatters entered and "tried the doors of empty huts till one opened . . . They took the first four rooms, two to each family, in an H-shaped hut already partitioned into 30 small bedrooms, two communal bathrooms . . . and one laundry room." The young men managed to turn on the water, but the barren rooms were without electricity and heat, and their mattresses had to be placed on the floor. Even so, their new quarters were preferable to their last ones in Gastown. Nellie Cox said, "It was terrible at Water Street... There were a lot of old men, and they would shout at us to shut up whenever the children made a noise." Cox was pleased that they could "turn around without wondering if the kids... [had been] killed by a car or truck." They made their first pot of coffee "with hot water borrowed from the Sergeants' Mess." Shortly after the squatters moved in, some of the army huts were turned over to the University of BC, where they were used as housing. Nine buildings were retained by the reserve army; six were allotted to the Department of Veterans Affairs. The *Province* noted that "trained social workers" were brought in to help squatters relocate, but the records do not indicate the fate of the Cox and Mooy families.

In 1950, a False Creek squatter, Frederick Roger Ducharme, was convicted of murdering a woman, and Vancouver ratepayers clamoured to have the shantytowns removed. In the *Vancouver Sun* of March 22, 1950, the squatters' homes were described as "disease-breeding, vermin-producing hovels;" the residents were said to be "unbelievably filthy" and a "nest of perverts." The *Daily Province* of October 3, 1951, however, described the majority of the squatters as "ordinary citizens."

Despite protests that the communities were health hazards and eyesores, most squatters managed to stay put. But in 1955, the False Creek squatters were issued their final eviction notice, as the site was required for a new government wharf. By June of that year only a few squatters remained. As Norman Hacking reported in the *Province*, they were the "last ditch survivors" and "the happy-go-lucky type." Some moved "just around the corner... to the other side of the bridge." For many, their homes were not worth moving; their choices were limited. One man lamented, "Try to find a house where me and the old woman can live on $40 a month." Another expressed concern that he might have to go back to his wife, who liked "beer parlours... If I move out tomorrow maybe she'll take me back. Maybe she won't. I hope she won't."

A community near Deep Cove, North Vancouver, was first inhabited by fishermen and employees of the Dollar Mill and McKenzie Derrick. Later, some of the jerry-built structures at Dollarton served as summer cabins for Vancouver families. For Malcolm Lowry and his wife, Margerie, life in a shack became an affordable refuge that removed Lowry from the temptation of beer parlours and liquor stores. Their 14 years as squatters provided Lowry with enough serenity to complete his most famous novel, *Under the Volcano*. He worked on other writings in the shack, including a book of short stories that received the Governor General's Award in 1961, four years after his death. The Lowrys' tenancy drew other writers such as Earle Birney, Dorothy Livesay and Al Purdy to the ramshackle beach homes. But the community was evicted in 1960, the shacks bulldozed and burned, and the foreshore became part of Cates Park. In 1958, eviction notices were given to the Burnaby squatters on the other side of the inlet; in 1960, the last members of that community moved and their shacks were destroyed.

Another Burrard Inlet squatter community sprouted on the Maplewood mud flats in 1971. Earlier squatters on the muddy estuary were forced out in 1961 when L&K Lumber purchased the property. Ten years later, hippies discovered the picturesque foreshore, moved in and set up tents, shacks and lean-tos. Some lived in vehicles. The BC sculptor Tom Burrows lived on the tidal flats for two years, taking inspiration from "the environmental setting, source of material, observation point (mainly the window of my cabin), the machinations of my squatter community, [and] the lunar rhythms of the tide."

The owners of the mudflats property, Lyttle Brothers Ltd., evicted the illegal tenants but reached an agreement with five people who were refusing to vacate. The firm agreed to pay them $500 "if they remove[d] a quantity of garbage" and moved. One occupant, 73-year-old Mike Bozzer, was allowed to stay because of his age. Bozzer had lived on the flats for 36 years. His four-room home was built from scrap lumber that had drifted onto the beach; so were

Malcolm and Margerie Lowry's third and final shack at Dollarton, North Vancouver, where they lived for 14 years. They moved here after their second home burned to the ground, taking with it the manuscript for Lowry's greatest work, *Under the Volcano*. *Photo courtesy UBC Library Rare Books & Special Collections, Fisherman Publishing Society*

his small veranda and his woodshed. Ironically, in 1980, the aged squatter himself had to evict his own squatter, a transient male who took up residence in his upstairs bedroom. Bozzer enjoyed his solitary existence until 1986 when, at the age of 88, he was forced by ill health to move to a care facility. The bulldozers were brought in and his shack was destroyed.

For 10 months in 1990, a group of people began occupying six empty houses on Frances Street in East Vancouver. Most of the squatters were homeless, young and single; a few said they were trying to escape "the rent rut." Others were "trying to make a point about housing, that this was good housing . . . and that it shouldn't be empty," according to John Shayler of the Tenants Rights Coalition. As many as 50 people at a time sought shelter in the buildings. In November, a violent confrontation took place between the police and the illegal tenants, "ordinary citizens on one side and . . . police and helicopters on

A fisherman tends his nets in Finn Slough, where a few of the 30-odd residents still work on gillnetters. Some say the settlement on Richmond's Gilmour Island is the oldest continuously working fishing community on the Fraser River.
Photo courtesy John Skapski

the other," in the words of Ald. Libby Davies. The squatters were arrested and city council ordered the homes demolished within 61 days. The owner said he planned to build 36 condominiums on the site.

Finn Slough, on Gilmour Island at the end of No. 4 Road in Richmond, has hosted squatters since 1892. Finnish immigrants were initially attracted by the beauty of the river flats, but the price of raw land was $40 an acre, a princely sum. The newcomers decided to build on Crown land and to fish the abundant waters of the Fraser River. Mikko Jacobson was one of the first, and built a scow-house to house his boat with a room at the back serving as makeshift living quarters. As more Finns heard about the community, the population grew, and in 1927, the municipality of Richmond ordered the occupants to pay property taxes or be evicted. Matti Lampi spoke for the squatters when he emphatically replied that as he was living on Crown land, he would not pay taxes.

A year later, the community moved 400 metres west. The new settlement became known as Finn Slough and, as Eric Sorila wrote, the scow-houses began "popping up like mushrooms in the rain." They were built with wood washed in by the river, or brought in by barge and horse-drawn cart from a sawmill in New Westminster. Residents added rooms to the scow-houses to make living in them more comfortable, "although a separate bedroom was... considered a luxury." Wood for heating and cooking was picked up along the riverbanks. Rainwater was collected for drinking and the river provided washing water. Saunas were an early and distinctive feature of the settlement. Washing machines and refrigerators were not acquired until 1959. Sewage went back into the river.

In the 1940s, the municipality again gave the residents notice to evict. According to Toivo Boren, the last of the Finns to leave the community, "the fishing company which bought the fish from the community fishermen became infuriated . . . because the fishermen were very productive and their evictions would mean less profit for the company." Thanks to the company's lobbying, the residents of Finn Slough were allowed to stay.

From 1950 to 1960, the population swelled to about 70 residents. But after 1960, the population began to decline, and from then until 1980, "funerals were the main social event" in the community. In 1984, municipal planners declared the community was unlikely to continue, in light of drainage problems and the fact that the area was zoned for agricultural, not residential, use. Nineteen years later, a community of about 30 individuals still exists. They are an eclectic mix including artists, pensioners and Vancouver business people. Like those before them, however, these residents are again threatened with eviction. A Toronto development company, Smith Prestige Properties Ltd., has proposed a multi-million-dollar development for the area.

Meanwhile, residents and concerned individuals have created the Finn Slough Heritage and Wetland Society. They want to protect the natural environment, to implement alternative methods of waste disposal for the community and to maintain an area for cyclists, walkers, equestrians, sports fishermen and naturalists. According to one resident, David Dorrington, those currently living at Finn Slough wish to preserve "the memory of how things were" in squatter communities. They see Finn Slough "as an important three dimensional, living part of that memory." To them "the village is not only a historical artifact . . . [but] an example of a possible way forward to find more creative solutions to . . . non-stop urbanization."

Should the Finn Slough homes and their inhabitants disappear in favour of suburban ranchers and townhouses, an integral part of the cultural and geographic history of the Vancouver area will be lost. Squatter communities will, however, always be a part of our heritage. In Malcolm Lowry's words, they will be remembered as symbols of "an indefinable goodness, even a kind of greatness." ◆

Sources and Further Reading

Burrows, Tom. Biography file, UBC Fine Arts Gallery (February 15, 1974).
Dorrington, David. "A Small History of Finn Slough." www.finnslough.com
Lowry, Malcolm. *Hear Us O Lord from Heaven Thy Dwelling Place.* New York: Lippincott, 1961.
Masson, Hal. "Sea-borne Shantytown," *Maclean's* (November 15, 1947).
Matthews, J.S. *Early Vancouver*, vol. 1. City of Vancouver Archives.
Sorila, Eric. "From Finland to Finn Slough." Unpublished paper, Richmond City Archives (1984).
Daily Province (Vancouver), Apr. 30, 1912; Nov. 17, 1923; Nov. 26, 1923; Oct. 29, 1936; Aug. 21, 1941; Aug. 26, 1941; Sept. 20, 1946; Sept. 25, 1946; June 14, 1955.
Province (Vancouver), Feb. 27, 1973; Nov. 28, 1990.
Vancouver Sun, July 25, 1953, Apr. 22, 1994.

NEVER SAY PIG

West Coast Fishing Superstitions

MICHAEL SKOG

"What the hell are ya bringin' that aboard for?"

That less than welcoming query came from a deckhand as I attempted to board a seiner, my arms loaded down with the bulging garbage bags and canvas duffels of the journeyman crewman. I was hoping to spend the summer salmon season replenishing my sorely undernourished bank account.

I was taken aback. I thought I had made a good impression the day before, my first with the boat's crew. I had shown up half an hour early and, over the course of the afternoon, sweated away two cans of Pepsi helping the seine net aboard and making other semi-voluntary preparations.

I silently reviewed every detail of the previous twenty-four hours, trying to figure out what I might

Illustration by Nick Murphy

have done to arouse this hostility. I followed the eyes of my accuser down my arm to the canvas gym bag containing my clean clothes.

"Ya can't bring a black bag on a boat. It's bad luck."

"This thing?" I asked, waggling the little bag dangling from my left hand. Being well past my rookie season on the boats, I knew about the black bag taboo, but I had always pictured a bad-luck bag as one that was black all over, like a black cat. This one had a colourful beer logo on it, and racing stripes. Only the background was black.

I was tempted to try arguing that this particular bag was not of the ill-omened variety, but what then? At the first sign that the trip was not measuring up, the blame would fall on my shoulders for packing aboard the Jonah bag. I would become the target of black looks and hostile silences, and nothing I could say about logos or racing stripes would do me the slightest good. I unpacked all my clothing and took the scorned object back to the car.

I have often had occasion to ponder just how it is that case-hardened skeptics who wouldn't entertain a supernatural thought if the archangel Gabriel visited them in person will nevertheless enforce the most bizarre shipboard taboos with the unshakeable conviction of a banker enforcing the terms of a mortgage. What is it that comes over normally rational people when they set foot on a boat, especially a fish boat? In the face of logic and science, they fall back on a primitive, warped logic: We observe these taboos and we're still alive, so the taboos must work. It's pure cause and effect.

Like every greenhorn eager to avoid the scorn of older hands, I once devoted a lot of brain volume to discovering and observing the superstitions of the trade. I concluded that the part of the cranium used to store this (dis)information must be the same area usually allotted to common sense, because the more superstitions one catalogues, the more difficult it becomes to resist even the most ridiculous ones.

The list is lengthy. Whistling is a widely forbidden activity. Years ago a shipmate told me to pipe down when he heard me unwittingly "whistling up the wind." Some forward-thinking people maintain that this prohibition applies only in the wheelhouse, but the prudent will stick to humming even these days, to be on the safe side.

Everyone has heard the saying, "Red sky at night, sailor's delight; red sky at morning, sailors take warning." But did you know that if you see a seagull taking a bath it means that the wind is about to howl? And if the gulls start moving inland it is really time to batten down the hatches.

Most will have heard of the proscription against leaving a hat on the galley table. The ban on opening the wrong end of a milk tin has also gained widespread notoriety. Less known is that the taboo applies to all food containers: All cans and boxes must be opened right side up or they have to be thrown over the side—no exceptions. Price is no consideration, so a tin of artichoke hearts gets tossed as fast as a can of consommé. Some interpretations of the dogma are stricter than others. One cook I sailed with threw out two jumbo cartons of milk in one week because he had inadvertently parted the waxed seal on the wrong side.

Today's fisherman stores most garbage in plastic bags atop the cabin instead of chucking it all overboard as in unenlightened times. But when this civilized practice comes head-to-head with the ancient juju about upside-downness, there is no contest. The defiled container is purged from the ship by the most direct route possible, as if it had suddenly become radioactive.

Many a hungry fishermen has come into the galley only to recoil in horror because some ignorant cook has roasted a turkey, otherwise known as "Blow Bird," or has laid before his crew a steaming bowl of pea soup, known as "Storm Soup." Whether it blows or not, few cooks make that mistake more than once.

Still on the subject of food, never, never mention the name of that low-slung, mud-loving animal that provides us with bacon. (Hint: it is a three-letter word which, enunciated backwards, sounds like "gip.") Refer to it only as "curly tail." Some crews enforce a ban against mentioning all barnyard animals by name. The extent of this farm-critter taboo differs from boat to boat. Some fishermen just bring up the superstition if such a word is used and laugh at it, as if it were a curious piece of trivia that might interest others, but the cautious greenhorn might be well advised to take a hint and avoid repeating the profane terms in any case. Sometimes it seems these taboos are falling into obscurity, but there is always an old-timer ready to infect the younger crew members and perpetuate the anxiety for another generation.

There is also a long tradition about not being entirely prepared for the best, as if that would be presumptuous in the eyes of fate. Large catches are what we are talking about, more fish than a crew knows what to do with. Everyone hopes for that big haul, and there are special bits of extra heavy tackle required if it comes. In salmon seining a brailer is needed for the biggest sets when there are too many fish to pull over the stern ramp.

But to prepare it beforehand is to ensure it won't be needed. Big hauls are more likely if the dipper is left down in the hole or "all confused in the rigging." The same goes for the other fisheries where the Boy Scout motto applies in reverse: Be not prepared, and maybe you'll be lucky enough to wish you were.

Then there is the dreaded hoodoo—a trade term describing any object or person believed to cause ill fortune. I have experienced the uncanny vibrations felt from these. One was another boat that caused us to pull in repeat water hauls (the seining equivalent of a "skunk") whenever it fished within sight. After we discovered the source of our bad luck we did everything possible to avoid this vessel, yet it continued to shadow us as if it knew its presence hexed us.

Superstition is probably linked in most people's minds with fear, and the most frequent explanation of ritualistic behaviour is that it is undertaken to ward off disaster. What this theory conveniently overlooks is that rituals intended to summon good luck are just as common as those intended to avoid bad. Maybe commoner. I have never actually seen a ritual being cooked up to ward off bad luck, but I've seen plenty of the other variety.

One of my skippers had a green baseball hat he insisted on wearing whenever he set the seine net. He'd been wearing it when he made his first big haul, and after that he wouldn't make a set without it, even though it was rancid with fish slime. He was convinced that the absence of that hat would be fatal to our hopes of a good season, and the entire crew shared that belief. We wouldn't let him take it off the boat, lest he forget it at home, or lest his wife—horror of horrors—launder it and remove its fishy mojo.

This kind of thing is common on the boats. I once wore a sour-smelling, sweat-marinated bandana to bed because I thought untying the knot would break a recent streak of good luck. Near asphyxiation from the stench eventually put an end to that, but most fishermen I know have fallen prey to similar quirks. Some compulsions run throughout the fleet like a collective neurosis. Most men don't shave or shower until the fishing trip is finished. Then there is the grand old belief that nothing bodes better for a prosperous trip than to have a dark-skinned woman come down and piss on the net. It's commoner than you might think, even today.

In fishing, where an entire season can be made in a single set, or lives may be lost in a single swell, there is much that remains beyond mortals' control. It is to avoid seeming totally helpless before these superhuman forces that fishermen cling to talismans and fetishistic rituals. A popular saying holds that there are no atheists in a foxhole. Neither are there unbelievers on the fishing grounds. ◆

ANGELS IN CAULK BOOTS

Tug Skippers in the Days Before Search and Rescue

DOREEN ARMITAGE

In addition to their regular chores of berthing ships and hauling booms and barges, BC's tugboats are often called upon to assist in emergencies, often working with the Coast Guard and fireboats to save lives and retrieve damaged vessels. In fact, until Coast Guard and Search and Rescue units were invented, tugs were the first—and sometimes only—help on the scene when mariners were in danger.

Two boys get a closer look at the *Unimak* as it is beached at Davis Bay August 7, 1960, more than a week after it sank off Gower Point. All four aboard were killed, the last trapped in an air pocket and banging on the hull as would-be rescuers looked on helplessly. Repaired and relaunched, the *Unimak* later collided with a tanker off Prince Rupert and went down for good. *Photo courtesy UBC Library Rare Books and Special Collections, Fisherman Publishing Society*

On March 6, 1945, the *Green Hill Park*, a 10,700-ton freighter, was loading at Pier B in Vancouver harbour. Longshoremen were stowing a variety of cargo such as newsprint, chemicals, distress signals, food and aircraft spare parts. Skipper Cyril Andrews and crewman Cec Phillips were awaiting orders on the Gulf of Georgia tug *Cuprite*, tied up at the BA Oil dock. Just before noon they received a phone call from their office directing them to go to the *Green Hill Park* and turn the lumber scow around. The men were finished loading from one side, and needed to have the scow turned so that they could reach the rest of the lumber.

The next few minutes would change the rest of Cyril Andrews' life.

"We went in there, and I had the deckhand letting go the lines off the scow. We were touching it and up against the *Green Hill Park*—and she blew. It sounded like a shot out of hell. When I saw the first explosion go straight up, it blew the hatch-tender with it. He went as high as the Marine Building and landed back on the deck. There were three blasts altogether and they blew me out of the wheelhouse every time. I had to be in close because there were men in the water and I had to get them out. The lumber barge was on fire, roaring away. We backed out away from it, and started pulling people out of the water. It was strange because we didn't know who they were. Men were climbing down ropes dangling from the ship's side, but were dropping like grapes from a vine at each explosion. I backed up to the dock and let the men off that we'd pulled from the water. A newspaper photographer jumped on board and went out with us as we looked for more survivors."

For most of the war Vancouverites braced for a Japanese attack that never came. Then on March 6, 1945, the freighter *Green Hill Park* blew up with enough force to shatter windows downtown. *Photo courtesy Doreen Armitage*

Debris was raining on buildings and streets. Pickles from the cargo fell like green hail. Hundreds of windows shattered in buildings from the waterfront to Georgia Street. Capt. Andrews continued: "We finally got the *Green Hill Park* away from the dock. Some people on the wharf had let the lines go. In the midst of the smoke and flames we pushed and pulled, then a bunch of boats came in to help. George Grey on the *Sumas* took the burning scow out into the middle of the harbour so we could get at the flaming ship. We got her pushed out a little bit, and turned her around. The *RFM*, a big tug, went in and put a line on her and started towing her out. We headed out of the harbour. She was turning this way and that and I was right alongside of her, pushing on her port side trying to keep her straight. We tried to put her on the beach where Vancouver Wharves are now, in North Vancouver, but the tide washed her off. She was burning furiously, and we didn't know if she was going to explode again or not. I said to my deckhand, 'I don't know if she's going to blow again.' We were only about 15 feet from her. 'Well,' he said, 'maybe we won't know this time if she blows.' They tried to stop us from pushing her under Lions Gate Bridge in case she blew and destroyed the bridge, never mind about us. The bridge controller was attempting to divert water traffic by shouting through his megaphone but no one could hear him. We finally got her up on the beach at Siwash Rock, and three fireboats pumped 35 feet of water in her over the next three days and nights to get the fire out.

"Afterwards Gulf of Georgia Towing provided the official boat for investigations. We were around there for about a week, with a representative from the underwriter firm Lloyd's of London. Every time a body was found he and I had to go up on board to verify its location. It wasn't a very nice job. In one place a guy had tried to climb up a ladder inside and he got caught. His arms were burnt off at his elbows, his legs were burnt off at his knees and his head was burnt off. He was hung on the ladder under his armpits."

The federal government investigated the disaster, and, based on available evidence, found that the explosion was caused by "improper stowage of combustible, dangerous and explosive material in No. 3 'tween decks and ignition thereof by a lighted match." The commission's assumption, confirmed years later by a deathbed confession, was that some longshoremen had broached barrels of overproof whiskey and dropped a match while attempting to illuminate the area. Flares stowed on top of the barrels ignited.

The explosion killed six longshoremen and two crewmen. Another 19 men were injured, and flying glass sliced into dozens of office workers. One serious injury not counted at the time incapacitated Andrews. Not realizing that he had a concussion, he couldn't understand what was happening to him later that month.

"I began having severe dizzy spells and collapsing. I hadn't known I had a concussion from being blown out of the wheelhouse. So the company took me off the tugs and I worked for the Towboat Owners' Association that had a hiring hall of their own called the Towboat Employment Agency at 220 Alexander Street in Vancouver. I couldn't work on a boat, but I needed employment. I was in and out of the hospital so many times and they were really trying to do something for me. I felt like I saw every doctor in the country. I was fed up with it. My head hurt so much. Everything would go black in front of me. One doctor told me it was all in my mind. An Air Force doctor took me on and worked with me for years and eventually got me halfway straightened out. They finally found out that my pituitary gland had been squashed by the explosion. I had to have an injection every day of my life for several years. I finally felt better."

In December, 1953, another disaster changed the course of search and rescue on the BC coast. Again, Capt. Andrews was involved. A tug called the *C.P. Yorke*, with eight crew, was running light up the coast one night. "The crew members were all good friends of ours," Cyril Andrews recalled. "We'd see them in the office regularly. Every time a crew would leave they'd come into the office and say, 'Hi you guys. Just saying hello.'" Only a few hundred yards from Secret Cove, going up through Welcome Pass, the *Yorke* hit Tattenham Shoal. Skipper Roy Johnson apparently wasn't too worried when the boat first grounded, expecting it to float off with the tide. But when a wild southeaster came up, the waves and rocks ground a hole in the hull. The *Yorke* rolled over and sank. There were several boats nearby, but in those days tugs' radios were usually tuned to music, probably *Bill Ray and his Roundup*. So they didn't know *C.P. Yorke* was in trouble as her mayday couldn't get through to them.

"The company sent me by car, and also a diver on a salvage boat, up there to search for bodies. I had a phone in the car, one of the first ones. I told George Unwin, who was the diver, that we'd meet him in Pender Harbour. Next day we went out on the boat looking for bodies. And we found six of them, unfortunately. The captain and engineer had made it to shore but it was the middle of winter. The engineer, who couldn't swim, had climbed onto the overturned lifeboat. Water kept washing over him. Freezing! Freezing! He had only pieces of the canvas cover for protection. Finally the boat washed up on shore, and he had to pull himself onto the beach with his elbows because his legs were paralyzed with the cold. Local residents found him and took him into the hospital in Pender Harbour. The captain was also found on the beach. He had a flashlight clutched in his hand, turned on. That's how they happened to find him. He was alive but unconscious. The nurse told me at the hospital that they

Views from a tug's deck as explosions rip through the *Green Hill Park*. Capt. Cyril Andrews recalls three explosions, 'and they blew me out of the wheelhouse every time.' *Photos courtesy Doreen Armitage*

had a terrible time prying the flashlight out of his hand. Both men came through all right. The rest died. We got the bodies and the boat. It was raised from about 80 feet of water by Straits Towing and was running again after a complete overhaul. This catastrophe, in my mind, is what started Search and Rescue. In those days the government wasn't willing to establish Coast Guard on the coast.

In December 1953, the tug *C.P. Yorke* sank in a storm in Welcome Pass. Six of its eight crew members died. There were other tugs in the area, but none of them heard the *Yorke*'s mayday—probably because they had their radios tuned to music programs. Cyril Andrews was determined to make sure that wouldn't happen again. *Photo courtesy Vancouver Maritime Museum*

"I thought, it's so ridiculous, all the boats have radios on them, but most of the crews are tuned to a music band and can't hear a mayday call. So I went to see my board of directors who were elected every year from the towboat companies, and I told them that I'd like to take all those radio bands with music on them out of the wheelhouses so the crews couldn't listen to music there, and put a radio in the galley for amusement. In the wheelhouse the radios would be tuned to 2182 kilocycles, the distress frequency. The directors thought that was a good idea, so the board sent out messages to all the companies about what they were going to do. And they did it in April 1954. Then we had framed notices made up for all the tugs with what to do in case of emergency and the steps to go through. Printed across the bottom was this: 'The life you save may be your own.'"

This marine rescue arm worked closely with the RCAF base at Jericho beach in Vancouver. Combined air and sea rescue services could be called on when necessary. Capt. Andrews was still working out of the towboat office but could not receive direct calls from the boats. Their mayday calls would go out to any government radio station that could pick them up, who then relayed them to Andrews on the radio telephone in the office, his car or his home. He then contacted any vessels in the vicinity of the accident and the captain of one of them was appointed search master. Andrews was on call 24 hours a day, and was not comfortable with the fact that the boats could not contact him directly. Finally he came up with a solution: "I used to go down to Second Narrows Bridge on my day off, and would sit and chew the fat with the boys while they were working. I thought: 'Their radio is only five watts, but why can't we use that?' So they got permission from their office for me to use it. But the government representative refused: 'You cannot use that radio, period!' But I said, 'I'm damn well going to use it.' He said, 'I'm ordering you.' But I told him I was going to use it anyway. After all, men's lives were at stake. He said it wouldn't reach up the coast but I asked him how come I could speak to the Coast Guard in Alaska on it. There was a write-up in the paper about the feud. Finally I asked Bob Cole what if someone jumped off the bridge or fell off a boat. Would I have to use a special lifebuoy to throw to that man in the water because we couldn't use your lifebuoys? There was a regular war going on, but I kept using the radio. Of course the towboat owners were behind me. The Second Narrows Bridge radio was a monitoring station and listening all the time. If something went wrong they phoned my office right away and I would jump into my car and boil on down to the bridge and use their station. Finally the rescue service got going so well that they formed a committee of companies involved. There was one representative each from the towboat owners, the pilotage, the CPR, Union Steamships, the Fishing Vessels Association, the CNR, Northland Navigation and me. They all agreed that if we needed any of their boats I had the authority to take them and use them; it didn't matter for how long, and for no cost. Nobody paid anything.

"We later went to the insurance companies and asked them what they were going to do to help us with our rescue efforts. They said, 'If you go to a rescue, first save the lives. But, if one of your tugs salvages the boat and tows it into Vancouver, we'll give you double the daily rate of the boat that's towing it.' The rate depended on the horsepower of the tug. For instance, if it had 1,500 horsepower they charged $1,500 an hour. But the insurance company cut down their insurance fees for those hours the guys were working on a salvage. But paying half of it was a good deal.

"The American Coast Guard liked it so much they came up here to see how we worked and we met with them once a month. We worked all over the province, even the lakes. If you were in distress you would switch to 2182 kilocycles and call 'mayday, mayday, mayday.' We had all the lighthouses on the same frequency. That's how it started, and it got so big that they decided that I shouldn't be in the towboat office; I should be in an office of my own. In the spring of 1956, the Department of Transport granted $10,000 toward my salary and some other expenses, and I was moved to an office at the Air Force base at Jericho. It was a highly secure building because it was the end of the radar line and was guarded. My past and my relatives had to be checked. I still hold the pass for it. It was a little awkward in a way because the Air Force didn't like a beastly civilian ordering them around. But I never really ordered them around; I was marine adviser to the Air Force. Then we went to the government to ask for marine telephones so I could talk to the boats to direct what was going on. They had a five-watt government station at Point Grey, so they hooked a line from that into my office, and when something happened I could talk to all the boats and the Air Force. It was so nice, because as soon as we had an emergency, I'd switch over to the 2366 frequency that all of the tugs talked to each other on, and say 'Hello the ships. Hello the ships. Hello the ships. This is Search and Rescue calling. This is a mayday call.' They'd all answer back. They were always rude to me, of course. On the waterfront you're always rude to each other. If you're not, there's something wrong. Jack Fish was a mate on the *Kenora*. I'd be on the air calling the ships and Jack Fish would call back 'We're out here, Curly [Andrews is bald]. What do you want us to do?' They'd give me their positions, and I'd check them on my huge chart.

"The Air Force boys were interested in plane rescues, but with me there they were also involved in marine rescues. No helicopters were used, just sea planes or wheeled aircraft. They would throw over lifesaving equipment, or lower a line and winch the people up. They did a very good job. The only trouble with the Air Force was that they had an hour's standby. You had to give them an hour's notice. I told the Air Force that it was wrong. You can't expect a guy to hold his breath for an hour. We found out from the doctors how long a guy could live in the water: they gave him at the best 30 minutes. So they brought the Air Force at Comox into it and they had a standby plane there at all times. The Air Force was always the one that spoke to the planes.

"When we got our boats lined up we always appointed a Search Master. He took the orders from me, although I never ordered, I always asked, 'Can you help?' I arranged for a moving line of boats ahead, and the Air Force would drop flares. L&K Lumber in North Vancouver gave us their airplane to use if we needed it. Larry and George Lyttle said I could have that plane anytime I wanted, with a pilot."

One highlight of Capt. Andrews' rescue efforts involved the disappearance of five men on the

Capt. Cyril Andrews

Hilunga, an 82-foot federal works department vessel. Capt. Herbert Dale-Johnson had radioed at 2:30 a.m. in a raging blizzard in February 1956: "I'm going to have to abandon ship. She's breaking up." He gave their location as Cape St. James, the southern point of the Queen Charlotte Islands. After one mayday call their radio was swamped. The Air Force sent planes out looking for any sign of the boat or the men, but after two days found nothing.

After the Air Force contacted him for assistance, Capt. Andrews took action. "I put out a call to any ship that had seen the *Hilunga*," he said. "The closest I could come was the report that one boat phoned in saying that he had seen it just about at the top end of Vancouver Island, and gave the day and the time. We worked out where that was, and I could calculate the speed of the *Hilunga* from the time it was seen to the time the captain got the distress out, the state of the tide and the weather, and there was no possible way she could be near Cape St. James. I drew an arc on the chart. If he had been on the port side of the arc he would have been in wide open seas. So he had to have been on the starboard side. I drew a mark across there and said, 'There it is, on Aristazabal Island, south of the Queen Charlottes.' When the Air Force went up the next day, there they were, on Aristazabal Island, waving from the rocks on the beach. The tug *Sea Monarch* picked them up that afternoon and they were transferred to a Canso rescue aircraft on the lee side of the island. It was very nice to get thank-you letters from the crew's wives. The *Hilunga* is still sailing. They brought her down to Vancouver and put a new bottom in her."

Despite his co-ordinated efforts, not all rescue attempts were successful. When, on November 10, 1954, the *Salmon Queen* sent out a distress call that it was sinking, Andrews had dozens of boats searching the Strait of Georgia near the mouth of the Fraser River for the missing fish boat with two crewmen aboard. "One boat, the *Master*, got it on his radar, but before the rescue boat could get there the signal disappeared. You know, they would load these wooden fish boats up with so much fish that the vessels would sink to below the regular water line, and, of course, the seams were open where the wood had dried out."

Capt. Andrews and the search and rescue team did enjoy some light moments during their serious searches. One day he requested assistance from some naval vessels in a search area. They radioed their position to the rescue team, who had difficulty interpreting it. "I finally sent a message to Victoria requesting confirmation of the latitude and longitude sent to us," Andrews smiled. "They agreed that it was correct.

"So I sent them a return message: 'Please confirm that the *Restigouche* is in Abbotsford.' That's what they had given us," he chuckled.

In 1960, the Dominion government began to make plans for a Canadian Coast Guard service, and

Capt. Howie Keast

the Department of Transport took over control of the West Coast marine search and rescue co-ordination after seven years of this successful service.

Capt. Howie Keast and Capt. Cyril Andrews were both present at the July 1960 sinking of the *Unimak*. Keast was also involved in the boat's salvage:

"We came across the gulf one night from Gabriola Island on the *Jean L.*, and we crossed over to [Cape] Roger Curtis. During our crossing we came across a fishing vessel heading for Vancouver, towing a reefer barge that carried canned fish and things like that, loaded up-coast. Just east of Gower Point, the vessel towing the barge had gotten into an accident with a fishing vessel called the *Unimak* that had crossed the stern of the tow vessel in front of the barge. Consequently the towline flipped the fishing vessel over, and it then caught up on the bridle gear. You can imagine the position that the skipper of the towing vessel was in. What do you do? Do you slow down? If you slow down it might sink. If you keep going you might hold it up. It was a difficult situation and a hard decision to make.

"As we were getting in past Roger Curtis with our log tow, a westerly wind had started coming up with a swell. There were several vessels including the CPR vessel *Princess of Vancouver* to give some assistance. Several tugs were in the vicinity and came to give a hand, but to no avail. These people in the boat were trapped upside down and had no way of knowing which way the boat was because of blackness. If the rescuers tried to cut a hole in the boat with a chain saw there was some chance that the vessel might sink because the air inside would escape. So with the swell, and increasing westerly wind, the vessel was getting lower in the water. You couldn't beach it properly because of all the problems with the masts, stay wires and so forth. Consequently the vessel sank, but had drifted far west of Gower Point towards White Islets. A diver named Frank Wright went down and tried to see if there was anything he could do. He found a girl but she was already drowned. The vessel took two men down, and there was little they could do in that situation."

Cyril Andrews: "God it was rough! The *Unimak*, a big fish boat, had hit a scow at night near Sechelt, and rolled over. Someone was banging from inside the hull. I brought in the CPR ship *Princess of Vancouver*, on its way from Nanaimo to Vancouver loaded with passengers, to make a breakwater beside the fish boat so that we would be able to get the guy out. We had quite a dilemma. We couldn't cut a hole in the bottom of the boat or it would go down as soon as the air came out. The only thing we could do was hope to hold it up and get a diver to go inside, a pretty risky move. The guy inside kept hammering away. It was a horrible feeling. The water was getting rougher all the time. The guys tried to string towlines between two tugboats and under the fish packer to hold it up, then we could run it ashore and cut a hole in the bottom. Of course we would still be taking the chance of hitting the fuel tanks, or steel plates. One of the rescue boats, the *Brentwood*, had a mast and derrick, and we hooked that up to the *Unimak*. It was so heavy that the weight tore the *Brentwood*'s mast out. All of a sudden the fish boat righted itself, then went down. We found out later that two men inside, and another man and a girl also drowned. That would have been a horrible death, in the dark—terrible. But what else could we have done? The CPR ship left then and proceeded to Vancouver. We had held up the transcontinental train for about six hours because they were waiting for the passengers. That was all okay."

Howie Keast: "A few weeks later we took on the job of salvaging the *Unimak*. We used a barge with a logging donkey from L&K Lumber, a Caterpillar and an arch that they used for hauling logs out of the woods. The grappling gear involved the barge, assisted by the *Kathy L.* and our tug, the *Jean L.* We had a big sweeping line going from the barge to our tug, and we dragged along the bottom in a large loop. When we thought that we had hold of something, we'd use what we called a haulback line attached to a logging block or shiv, which would tighten up the loop and go around the vessel, or whatever we had hold of on the bottom. Then we would haul up what was attached. Eventually we found the *Unimak*, but we didn't know what we had ahold of. So we brought it up and the RCMP patrol vessel gave us a hand with their depth-sounder to show us the best way to get in to the beach. While we were holding this vessel just below the surface of the water, we used an inch-and-an-eighth cable, which was rubbing on the angle iron on the barge's bumper. The steel stranded the cable and it broke. Back down goes the vessel. It was so heavy. The wood was just saturated, impregnated with water, and it was down 450 feet, very deep to find without using electronics. We checked the amount of water pressure later with someone at UBC who said it was 198 pounds per square inch, so you can imagine the pressure that was on it. When we did get ahold of it the first time a lot of the penboards floated to the surface. They're eight feet long, six or eight inches wide, two inches thick and used for making various pens for fish in the hole of the fish boat, and they were just barely floating. A propane tank came flying up from the bottom and blew off all the propane, and gallon cans came up that were squished, crushed together. There was a lot of pressure there.

"So after losing the boat, and trying for the second time, we rearranged our grappling gear, and shortened up the line to the logging donkey to give us a better purchase on the winch. We caught the boat again, and this time we brought it up and held it. The sweeping line must have come up over its stern and the loop tightened on the drag boards cabled to the deck. They are used on fishing boats to drag along the bottom, attached to the fishing nets that are above and behind them. We were worried that the boards would come loose. If our line had come up over the bow, it would have slipped off over the stay lines. We took it in to Davis Bay at Sechelt, beached it, and waited for higher water to float it further in. In the meantime we got some barrels from the Chevron at Sechelt and put them in the fishing hole of the vessel. They helped to give it more buoyancy at the next high water. When the tide came in we moved it in a little further and when the tide went down the RCMP were there to get the bodies out. This was a Sunday morning, and the priest came down and told me that we had a bigger congregation than he did at the church. We patched the boat up and towed it into the shipyard at Coal Harbour. It was repaired and went back to sea again. However, the last I heard of that vessel was that it was hit by an Imperial Oil tanker up off of Prince Rupert and went down with no loss of life. But the boat went down and never came up again.

"I still have a shotgun and a lifebuoy as mementos from the *Unimak*. The shotgun today is rusty, I would never use it, but it is a treasure. We found out later that the *Unimak* was one of the deepest wrecks on the coast brought up to the surface without electronics to aid in locating." ◆

Oar, Paddle and Sail

Nineteenth-Century Transit Along the BC Coast

Lynn Ove Mortensen

Intricately decorated ceremonial canoes are rafted together to form a floating stage for potlatch dancers at the home of Chief Wakas of Alert Bay. This totem pole stood for years at Stanley Park in Vancouver before it was restored and installed in the Canadian Museum of Civilization. *Painting by Gordon Miller, courtesy Canadian Museum of Civilization*

Well into the 20th century, movement around the British Columbia coastline relied on oar, paddle and sail. Even after the advent of scheduled steamer routes and outboard engines, most people depended mainly on human power and the whim of the wind for everyday travel.

Small boats were the workhorses of the coast and one of the cheapest and most available forms was the Native canoe, hand-hewn from local cedar. Pioneers often bought dugouts or, for money or trade goods, hired them, complete with Native guides who acted as navigators, translators and/or fellow paddlers.

Coastal lore brims with tales of robust rowers and lengthy journeys. Skookum Tom Leask of Quadra Island rowed to the Queen Charlottes and returned with a bride. Hans "the Boatman" Hansen lost a hand in a hunting accident while working at Hastings Mills in Vancouver. Undaunted, he had a hook fitted to his arm, which connected into his oars. Finally settling at Port Neville on Johnstone Strait, Hansen thought nothing of rowing and sailing to Vancouver and back again for supplies or medical care when necessary. Once he offered a friend a ride home. The friend thought he'd reach Port Neville faster on the Union boat but Hansen arrived first and was there to greet him when he stepped ashore.

Ernest Halliday explored the coast by rowboat in search of a farm for his wife and two children and finally settled on expansive meadows near the mouth of Kingcome Inlet. Nearing the arrival of her third child, Lilly Halliday helped Ernest row from Kingcome to Comox for the baby's delivery. The trip lasted 14 days and the small family was forced to negotiate Seymour Narrows in a blinding snowstorm.

Contemporary accounts of these remarkable feats speak of time elapsed, weather and blisters, but rarely describe the sights, sounds and smells travellers encountered. We hear little about their supplies and gear, their impressions of the countryside through which they passed or the problems

Snuneymuxw (Nanaimo) band paddlers pose behind the *Patricia*, an 11-man racing dugout.
Photo courtesy Snuneymuxw First Nation

caused by cultural and language barriers. Most were too busy eking out a living to leave chatty written records. Fortunately, several unusually detailed accounts of early travels along the coast remain to lend glimpses of what these early trips were really like.

In the spring of 1862, Reginald Pidcock, barely 21, arrived from England with several other upper-middle class young men to try his luck in the Cariboo goldfields. Six years later, Pidcock wrote the story of his first year in the new colony. Its immediate tone and attention to detail—if not to spelling—seem to indicate that he'd kept a journal.

While Pidcock's upbringing and status certainly influenced the quantity and quality of his initial supplies, his packing lists suggest an idea of goods available in Victoria and contemporary advice for such an undertaking. Pidcock's later revisions reflect practical adjustments learned from experience.

At that time, well-off travellers surrounded themselves with a sea of trunks, bags and luggage of every kind. Even before he left Victoria for the Cariboo, "Pid" had some misgivings about his travelling gear:

> In starting for a Colony... I should advise every one to take nothing but a very portable portmanteau as boxes and other baggage are a source of great expense and trouble & hinder & delay in a most terrible manner... & then half the contents is useless & the other half seems too good for the Country.

Pid advised "several pairs of strong lace up boots with good knitted stockings, two or three suits of good tweed of a grey or light brown colour... but a good gun or rifle is indesspensible [sic]."

After a brief, unsuccessful foray toward the Cariboo, Pidcock and friend Harry Blaksley backtracked to Victoria, concocting plans for a canoe trip up-island. They hoped to reach Comox, the new island settlement fast becoming an important northern outpost. By then Pid had rethought his supplies.

"We invested in a blanket shirt apiece... the very best thing to travel & hunt in... & we took a half dozen flannel shirts & two pair of fustian trousers, as these last stand the ware & tear of the bush better than Cloth." The strong cotton-linen twill, usually with a pile face, may have bettered Pidcock's original tweed, but still would have been very weighty, especially when wet. The young men wore "rather heavy lace-up boots" when venturing ashore, but soon learned to make Native-style rawhide moccasins for hunting and paddling, "as a Canoe will not bear to be roughly used."

They bought a dugout and made a sail, which would double as a handy addition to "Indian mats to lie on & also to form a . . . tent . . . We bought two pair of heavy blankets, two light axes, a frying pan, & some tin pots or 'billies' . . . to boil & stew in . . . . "

Provisions included four or five bags of flour, bacon, salt, pepper, yeast powder, and whisky. Hot grog proved "a great treat . . . if we had got very wet during the day." They carried a rifle, "double barrel gun" and a good stock of powder and lead to insure fresh meat. Pidcock's rifle stood four feet, 10 inches in length. It weighed 12 pounds and had a hair trigger. He also carried a thin, easily sharpened sheath knife to use for every purpose, "either skinning a dear, or eating ones meal or cutting a stick."

The adventurers set out on a "fine morning in September . . . We had to start early . . . to catch the tide which runs very strong just outside Victoria & for many miles beyond . . . " Pidcock records passing Natives trolling for salmon, digging and drying clams, which he and Blaksley relished.

> It is a Curious sight to see a party of Indians moving about. If only going to a short distance for a short time they do not move their houses but take their boxes and all their goods and chattels including, cats, dogs & children all stowed away in a wonderful manner, with their brass kettles of which they are very fond. Large mats of different descriptions some made of Cedar bark others of very large Rushes . . . form very comfortable mattresses . . . and also make capital dry & warm huts to live in. They travel very slowly in Summer time . . . and sing a Sort of monotonous Chant which is heard at a great distance in Calm weather.

A party of Natives heading for Nanaimo warned the pair that Dodd Narrows were "hyas skookum" or very strong. Pidcock's account shifts into the present tense as he recalls the excitement of the crossing:

Moving between seasonal fishing grounds or visiting relatives, coastal Natives routinely take the entire family, household goods and all, aboard the dugout. *Photo courtesy Snuneymuxw First Nation*

Dugout canoes, whether the ocean-going whalers and war canoes pioneered by the Haida 1,000 years ago or smaller versions for everyday use, required weeks or months of highly skilled craftsmanship to construct. Recognizing their superiority as 'commuter' vessels for coastal travel, 19th-century Europeans commonly hired or bought Native dugouts.
Photo courtesy Maritime Museum of BC

> The tide had just begun to run against us . . . it was a question whether to try it or not but as our Indian friends wanted to get through and we should have to wait till next morning if we wanted daylight . . . we determined to try it. The Indians gathered themselves together and paddled all the time. [We] put our best hand forward and prepared for the struggle. Now we are in the middle of it paddling for our lives, the Indians strain every nerve and give a shout to every stroke. We make hardly any headway and all at once the canoe is caught by a strong eddy & back we both go like lightening & have some trouble in keeping clear of the rocks. Now we try it again always keeping in the wake of the Indians & with a tremendous shout and great straining we hold our own and stand quite still so strong is the current, until another whirl comes and we make a desperate effort and are through . . .

While they were camped at Nanoose Harbour "two canoes, attracted by the smoke of our fire came over to see who we were . . . They asked for a little tobacco and seem very much pleased when we gave them each a small piece & offered us some oysters . . . not anything at all equal to our English oysters either in size or flavour."

With some difficulty Pidcock shot a deer. Stumbling under the load, the novice hunter managed to get it back to camp. "The beast was very fat & weighed . . . 80 or 90 lbs." Blaksley meanwhile had cut firewood, shot a goose and several ducks, and cooked supper. "We had a most comfortable camp and sat rather late over our fire."

In Victoria the men had learned to make thick beds of evergreen boughs to achieve "a nights rest as it is not the lot of many persons to enjoy." Amid other nighttime sounds like "porpoises blowing & seals crying . . . " Blaksley awakened Pidcock to a "chorus of the most doleful yells . . . which made us both put our hands to our guns & sit up. The howling proceeded from a pack of wolves who had no doubt followed on my trail . . . I never heard such a melancholly noise in all my life . . . "

In the morning they feasted on "venison steaks and kidneys . . . then cooked some bread with yeast powder stowed all again in the Canoe and started off."

In 1884, the Norwegian B. Fillip Jacobsen arrived on the BC coast to collect "artifacts & curiosities" for European display. Barely 20, he had much experience under his belt. Under the command of his 14-year-old brother Adrian, six-year-old Fillip had helped pursue shark livers off Norway's northern coast. As a teen, he again followed Adrian's lead, becoming a curio collector for a German zoological firm.

Starting along Pidcock's route, Fillip "...took a canoe and one Indian...on my collecting trip..." When the wind was right, they hoisted a sail made from flour sacks still bearing colourful advertising labels. This amused Jacobsen and "...the Indian was...very much pleased with it as it was a regular picture gallery all through."

The Natives' stores seemed even leaner than Pidcock's. They carried bacon, beans and rice; but breakfast and dinner often consisted of salmon cooked the Native way, splayed between sticks angled over a fire, which Fillip "got to leike...very much..."

Jacobsen spoke no English and met few white men along the way "...but the Indian was talking chinok [Chinook] to me all the time and by the time we richet Allert Bay I was fair in chinok...and there for when I meet a whiteman...I tolket chinok."

Alert Bay was as far as his Native companion had agreed to go, so Jacobsen found a Native family to accompany him through the intricate maze of waterways leading from Broughton Strait. Here lay villages steeped in the rich traditions of the Kwakwaka'wakw culture. Because it was forbidden to part with dance masks, rattles and other ceremonial regalia, he traded secretly at night at Mamalilaculla and nearby villages. Here also he learned that sharply-pointed Kwakwaka'wakw paddles, made of stout yew, doubled as spears.

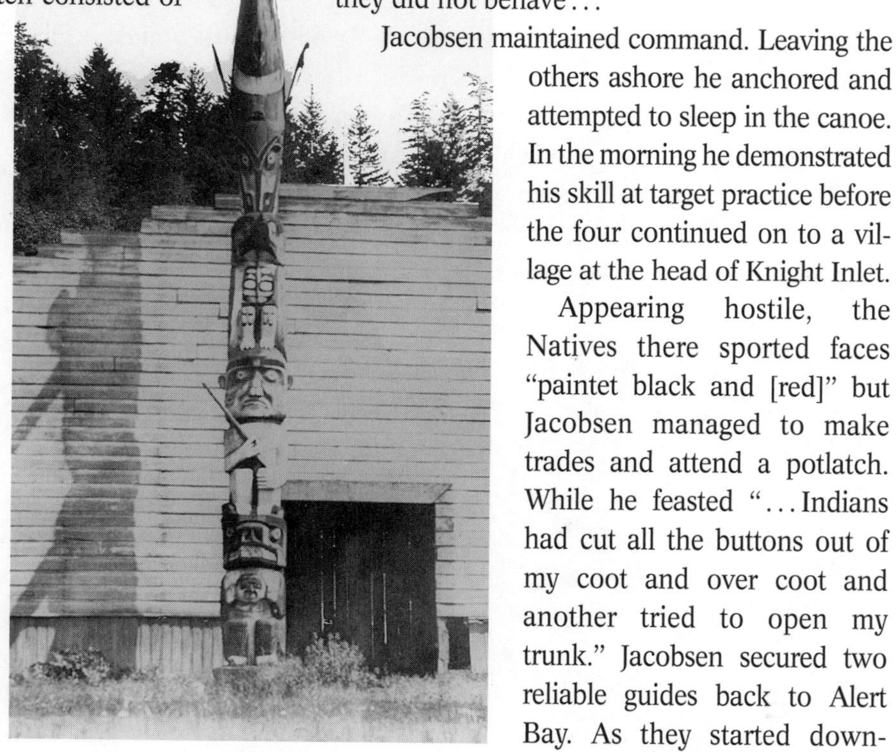

During their coastal travels, Pidcock and Jacobsen would often stay overnight at Native settlements such as this one at Cape Mudge on Quadra Island. Relations between Natives and whites could be unpredictable, however; Jacobsen claimed his life was threatened by his paddlers.

Adrian had suggested great caution in this region. Paddling up Knight Inlet with an old woman, her son and teenage grandson, Filllip grew apprehensive. The woman muttered a steady stream in Kwakwala, and near evening the others began sharpening their paddles.

Finally, Fillip recognized a signal; "like lightening" they attacked...Fillip drew his "6 shotter and...they got so scaret that they droppet right down in the canno. I could not swer in Chinok as there is not such a word, but I certainly told them whot I would do to them if they did not behave..."

Jacobsen maintained command. Leaving the others ashore he anchored and attempted to sleep in the canoe. In the morning he demonstrated his skill at target practice before the four continued on to a village at the head of Knight Inlet.

Appearing hostile, the Natives there sported faces "paintet black and [red]" but Jacobsen managed to make trades and attend a potlatch. While he feasted "...Indians had cut all the buttons out of my coot and over coot and another tried to open my trunk." Jacobsen secured two reliable guides back to Alert Bay. As they started downstream in a downpour, a mudslide rolled into the canoe, splitting the bottom. The men managed a quick repair and continued through relentless, heavy rain. Coming up the inlet, Fillip had noticed a small house. Drenched, they beached nearby as dark fell, and gobbled "dry salmon and water sooket hard tack."

Anticipating a dry night's rest, Jacobsen headed for the tiny house, but he couldn't convince his companions to join him. Not finding a door, he clambered through a loose board and

> laid myself down to sleep... but mighty litle did I have on account of the wet blanket. When daylight com... to my astonishment I noted the leg bone of a skeleton stiking trough the end of one of the boxses... I had sleept in an Indian grave house.

While Pidcock paddled the coast for pleasure and Jacobsen for profit, a third early traveller made a canoe trip for very different reasons:

In April of 1880, 26-year-old Helen Kate Woods set out with her younger brother Edward to visit their older sister, Alice, wife of Robert Tomlinson, the Anglican missionary in Ankihtlast, near Kispiox. Irish born, Helen Kate was raised in comfortable circumstances in Victoria, unaccustomed to the kinds of challenges she was to face—especially the intense cold.

Dugouts were remarkably seaworthy in the hands of expert paddlers. Here two Egmont men brave Skookumchuck rapids. *Harbour Publishing photo*

Kate and Edward left Victoria aboard the *Otter* bound for Kincolith, where they rested and prepared for a trip up the Nass River and overland to the mission. After provisioning and despite some misgivings about bad weather, the small party left against a strong wind at 2 p.m., "when the tide would serve." The Natives of the village, gathered to bid them farewell, wondered "much at my strong heart."

"[T]hrough rough water we forced our way for about three hours... had it not been for the extreme cold, the journey so far would not have been disagreeable," she wrote. Around 7:30 they encountered ice. Arthur, the head Native guide, explained they must lift the canoe and contents on to sleighs. Following Arthur's instructions, they walked "by the side of the canoe, holding on to it... Most places [the ice] was soft, plashy thaw stuff—we sank sometimes five or six inches..."

After about an hour a smell "steals slowly, gently—not sweetly—over our tired senses." It was "... the refuse of the Indian 'river harvest' of fish, fish oil and grease. I never did so heartily enjoy a bad smell!... We can see... bright fire lights shining through door-ways and walls of [Native] houses..."

Stopping at a fish station "established by our countrymen... our first care is to make tea. TEA—hot from a billycook and sipped from tin mugs—it is life, strength, rest, refreshment—all in one..." After the Woods' first night of roughing it, the cannery workers served up a breakfast of "porridge carried round in a huge milk pail... small fish and fried potatoes, hot rolls, bread and coffee and last but not least, a large china washing basin full of dried apples and peaches stewed together."

Morning presented even worse travel conditions. With a cry of alarm, Arthur and the sleigh broke through. Helen Kate had been quite

Nearly a month after leaving Victoria, the intrepid Helen Kate Woods and her brother arrived at remote Ankihtlast, where their older sister and her husband ran a mission—depicted here in a sketch by Kate.
Illustration courtesy BC Museum and Archives

close to Arthur and was splashed with the freezing water. She "thought it safer to abandon the canoe and keep as close along shore as possible, and so hand in hand with a [Native] woman named Catherine I make for the shore, jumping... from hummock to hummock of the rough ice."

> The difficulty now is to get the bow-sleigh out of the hole... [which is] only accomplished by hauling the canoe back far enough to free the sleigh. In doing this the stern sleigh breaks through, Edward going... with it... not an encouraging omen for the beginning of our journey.

This day's trip presented strange sights. "We met a sleigh piled with packages and boxes, on top of which an Indian woman sits holding a pole in her hand as a mast, on which was stretched an old black petticoat as a sail... while her husband (ran) behind" with a rope to guide it, "the wind and the petticoat carrying it forward."

Reaching solid ice, the men packed Kate "in the middle of the canoe with tents and blankets rolled round me while the snow-shoes were arranged fan-wise to shelter me from the wind." The men "rush along full speed, jumping, running and shouting..."

Helen Kate recorded the dress of some Native women in a village they passed:

> Their feet were encased in moccasins, the blanket leggings fitting nearly tight, then blanket skirts reaching to the knees, and a blanket jacket of many colours; it being not unusual to see the front of a jacket made from a scarlet blanket while the back will be green and the sleeves of an ordinary white blanket—then outside of all a blanket worn as a shawl or a marmot robe 'skinny side out, woolly side in'—with blanket hoods closely covering the head and greater part of the face.

At the end of the ice, tea was prepared "in the shelter of an Indian house as it was blowing too hard to prepare anything outdoors." They canoed on in open water until 7:30 p.m. when they reached their camping ground. "Having first cleared away the snow to the depth of about two feet we pitched our tent, spread dry branches" in front and "lay with our feet towards the fire while supper was being prepared."

In the morning, they "took to our canoe again, the river here being narrow and very swift it took all our strength to paddle and pull up . . . toward evening it grew intensely cold and threatened snow." Helen Kate and Edward hoped to camp out rather than sleep in the nearby Indian village, but Arthur advised them to seek the "shelter of a roof."

> Settled in the house selected for us, we set about preparing supper as quickly as we could, being somewhat afraid of having a meal prepared for us, which Indian etiquette would not have permitted us to decline . . . The house was about forty by fifty feet all in one room, and each occupant sat or stood or lay down just where he or she liked—Edward and I lay apart towards the top of the room, wrapped in our blankets. [The Native guides] lay on the floor but carefully within the four posts of a bed-stead from which all the laths have been removed. The "use" of the bedstead had been offered to me but I had declined . . . .
>
> I found in this my first night in an Indian house plenty of warmth, pure air, and no bad smells. To prevent ashes from the open

Reginald Pidcock became the prosperous and respected patriarch of a prominent family in the Campbell River area, and his offspring inherited his passion for paddling. Here Herbert Pidcock takes the King of Siam fishing.
Photo courtesy Museum at Campbell River

> fire falling on my head I made a cap of one of Edward's red handkerchiefs... and I more than once asked myself "What would folks at home have thought had they seen me that night?"

The next day navigation proved still more difficult and Arthur, who "having hurt his feet... felt he would not be up to the work on the trail which we now must take to. We were fortunate in finding a Skeena Indian to take his place."

Soon after, the party reached ice again. Edward and one of the guides fell through, getting so wet they determined to stop even though it was still afternoon. The camp was an old Chinese stopping place on the trail to the Omineca. There was firewood cut and dry branches for bedding. The guides found a Chinese shoe and spent the evening imitating "the chatter of Chinamen" as well as performing "tricks of strength and skill." The next morning they left the canoes, dividing the stores and gear, and started up the river.

Their hike over the rugged grease trail to Tomlinsons' mission at Ankihtlast lasted from April 17 to April 29 and provides a story of dogged hardiness all its own.

Helen Kate planned to stay only for the summer but weather prevented her return to Victoria until the following year. She married in 1882 and remained in that city until her five children were grown. Reginald Pidcock originally settled in Comox and became a respected leader among the upcoast villages. And Fillip Jacobsen, who continued his collection of artifacts as far north as Tongass, Alaska, returned to homestead in the Bella Coola Valley. ◆

Reginald Pidcock eventually settled in the Comox area, becoming an Indian agent and, as this photo of his estate shows, a prosperous landowner.

Source Notes

Faa, Eric. *Norwegians in the Northwest.* Funestad, 1995.

Pidcock, Reginald Heber. "Adventures in Vancouver Island. Being an Account of 6 years residence and of hunting & fishing excursions with some Account of the Indians inhabiting the Island." 1868. BC Archives. Add Mss 0728, Vol 4.

Woods, Helen Kate. Diary, Spring 1880. BC Archives Add Mss 773.

The Lightkeeper and the Crow

Pete Fletcher

Being a lightkeeper should have been a contemplative job, and so it was but for a few irritants: a shortage of fresh reading material, an always-empty larder, severe water restrictions... and that bloody crow.

East Point lighthouse perched on a cliff's edge at the end of a long finger of land protruding from Saturna Island's eastern shore. An American lightstation, Patos Island, faced us across five kilometres of boiling ocean, Boundary Pass. It was a cauldron of churning tidal upwellings streaming back and forth with sudden rushes. Talkative persons, not valuing the moment and wishing to compete with nature, would often have to shout above the roar.

The sea here is deep. A drop-off of 37 fathoms was half a stone's throw from the kitchen window. As a consequence, waving at the crew of deep-sea freighters was commonplace, our own goodwill effort. We exchanged fractured languages, big smiles, and friendly gestures. I recall one Russian freighter passing close by, its crew lined up on deck doing calisthenics; in a quick rush their ranks broke. Twenty good-natured seamen were calling out cheers and flailing their arms in greeting. Lining up in front of

Fervently I waited for departure day—a day that never came . . . Plainly, he had settled in for a lengthy visit. *Illustration by Carolyn Houg*

The ghost of East Point's original wooden tower, demolished in 1967, is superimposed over the open-frame metal tower that replaced it. The light was automated in 1996. *Illustration by Graham Scholes*

the tower in fine military fashion, my wife, my son, my daughter and I waved our jackets in response. It was a grand spot—the centre of the universe, at least to me.

Our house was a tired veteran built in 1888. Once its peak had sported a lantern, but that had been relocated to a steel tower and the roof closed over. It was cold and drafty and flying a flag indoors during a breeze was no great trick. But it was home.

Nature was the backdrop to each day, and my bonds with the old girl had always been deep. My acquaintance with crows, for example, had always been cordial. Their comings and goings could be noisy, but on the whole, we got along. Privately, I considered them the motorcycle gang of the bird world. But that was just a thought.

On a day of ill fortune I found a bald sausage stuck with pin feathers under a fir tree. Fallen from the family nest, it was a squawking baby crow.

A picture of nursing and nourishing clouded my reason. A scene appeared, in soft water-coloured, fairy-dusted splendour, depicting an adult bird, released, flying free with a thankful heart beating praise for my kindness. I picked the bird up and carried it to the house.

Immediately, I was faced with a feeding problem. Food stocks were sparse at the best of times. Supply tenders sent to revictual the station were, at that period, infrequent and unreliable. Canned food was the family staple, augmented by meat, fowl and seafood taken from nature's larder at the back door. So a balance was struck. I fed the ugly fledgling on bread soaked in tinned milk, dog food, which became his favourite, and strips of venison and rock cod. He flourished.

Anyone who has stood beneath a tree listening to the incessant begging for sustenance which makes up a young crow's life will appreciate the demands now placed upon my time. Any movement in the house—a door being opened or closed, a pot rattled, or perhaps a sneeze—brought a clamour from the cardboard box by the kitchen woodstove. Turning on the foghorn or closing the gate outside would produce the same result. I became a creature of stealth, padding about in bare feet, even tiptoeing quietly from room to room. Objects were picked up in slow motion, carefully, with firm grasp, so as to allow no sound to trigger the raucous demands that would surely follow.

When at last he became fully fledged I removed him to the outdoors. Thankfully I watched him learn to fly. Fervently I waited for departure day—a day that never came. Having grasped the rudiments of flight, he now possessed the ability, and most certainly the inclination, to follow me. Everywhere. Appearing suddenly from an empty sky he would alight upon my shoulder and issue his catalogue of requirements. I had my own feathered Walkman. Plainly, he had settled in for a lengthy visit.

Seconds after the smiling pose was recorded on film, the crow would suddenly clamp his beak on the soft earlobe of his host.
Photo by Pete Fletcher

Trolling for salmon one pleasant summer's day, I was interrupted by an ominous silhouette. Moments later I had a crow on the cabin top. He cast covetous eyes on the herring strip lying on the stern seat. He made a half-hearted grab for it and I waved him off. Just then the bell on one of the cedar poles jingled. A fish! And while I was engaged hauling in the hand line and securing the all-important supper, he quickly saw his opportunity and made off with the bait package and all its contents.

It was the opening salvo in what would be a long and troublesome war. And what a one-sided contest it was.

He had a peculiar habit that became more noticeable with time. When deeply satisfied with himself, as he often was, he would hunch over in low profile, white lids blanking out his eyes. Thus sightless, he would bob up and down chortling with a "nyuk, nyuk, nyuk" identical to the snicker of Curly of Three Stooges fame—except that it was steeped in malice, as I was to learn.

Underneath the open-framed steel light tower lay a large pile of fine sand intended for a future project. My four-year-old son had constructed a miniature world of mountains, ravines, lakes, tunnels, bridges and roads, all nestled in the bosom of this inviting mound. Along these roads travelled his much loved collection of metal cars and trucks. Matchbox toys, as they were called, were highly prized collectibles and the very centre of this young lad's life.

Swooping down from the rooftop, the crow selected a splendidly-painted, red double-decker bus. He poked his beak through the passenger windows and fled with the prize. His next move was hard to witness. As straight as the storied crow flies he flew out to sea and dropped his plunder. A tiny splash below marked the spot. Returning, he landed on the clothesline where he bobbed about in a self-congratulatory rhythm. His young victim burst into tears. Despite a careful watch, the four-wheeled fleet was soon decimated. A few survivors were moved indoors, and the once bustling metropolis on the sandy hill fell silent. The crow cast about for further adventure.

Saturna Island's dry climate made potable water a carefully rationed commodity. Rainwater was funnelled from the roof into a meagre 5,500-litre concrete cistern. For a family of four, especially one with young children, this was a pitiful amount. The taps were turned on with care. Bathwater was shared. Seawater was hauled up the cliff in buckets for the toilet. Washdays were critical exercises in cleaning the maximum piles of clothing with the minimum amount of water.

Sitting inside eating lunch one washday, we were interrupted by the dreaded sounds of sinister chuckling. They were coming from the clothesline outside the screen door. On examination of this sure-to-be-crime, we found all the wet, freshly cleaned laundry lying in heaps upon the dusty ground. One by one, working with devoted dedication, the crow had pillaged his way along the line, releasing clothes pegs as he travelled.

It came to be that with all future washings, one family member was assigned as a broom-waving sentry. And what a rigorous occupation it was too; calling for speed and precision as well as cunning and dexterity. The foe's interest in the gleaming wash never diminished. Frequently, flagging guards had to be relieved due to exhaustion.

Painting season at the lighthouse meant that all the nine buildings that made up the station were to be painted white, and the roofs red. It was a big job, made harder by the constant intrusion of a feathered nuisance. He developed a knack for judging when a paint can was empty enough, and consequently unstable enough, that he could perch on its edge and tip it over. As summer progressed, he took on a colourful red and white coat. He also liked to roost on freshly painted spots where he could mince back and forth to ensure a continuity of blemishes. For awhile he looked like a skunk, sporting a broad white stripe on his back where I had flung a paint brush at him.

One day while I was mowing the pathetic patches of grass we called a lawn, a rock flew out and shattered a large pane of glass in an engine room window. Scouring the supply shed, I discovered I did not have another pane, or a piece large enough to cut. So I boarded up the window and set out on the long trek to buy a replacement.

East Point was 18 kilometres by road from a ferry terminal, small grocery store, post office, and that most vital of all links, a telephone. Calling the narrow clearing through the trees a road was really stretching it. No rock fill or ballast had ever been used in its construction. As a result the dirt had been worn into deep ruts, a railway as it were, where one could take the hands off the steering wheel and motor slowly along enjoying the scenery. Usually the trip took an hour and a half each way.

I phoned the hardware store on Saltspring Island and ordered the glass. Making further arrangements, I asked the mate on the ferry to look after my fragile cargo, and met the vessel the following day to pick it up.

With the new pane at the ready, I proceeded with repairs. Cleaning out the old putty, I carefully scraped a flat surface for the new. The pane was then held in place by freshly moulded sealant around the frame.

Inside the workshop, I was hammering the lid back on to the can when I was startled by the noise of breaking glass.

Running out to the engine room I was just in time to see the crow fly off with a long strip of putty in his bill. He had managed, by dint of evil industry and an ability to hover like a hummingbird, to remove it all. My new glass lay in ruins at my feet.

I kept a boat moored on the Tumbo Channel side of the light, where its exposure to westerly breezes caused many an anxious night. Even more worrisome was the temperamental engine, a sullen lump of metal that required constant upkeep. I despised it, catered to it, and kept it alive.

Removing the cylinder head one day and tinkering with the petulant innards, I realized I needed a few more tools. Rowing the skiff back to the beach I saw the black shape of my arch-enemy entering the boat. My first thoughts were for the welfare of the shiny new, chrome-clad, open-end wrenches. I have broad shoulders, having grown up in a watery world where I learned to row at about the same time I learned to walk. I cranked the skiff around in its own length and flailed those oars. The skiff was planing by the time I arrived back alongside. But it was too late.

Ignoring all the enticing plunder lying about the deck, the crow had selected instead the cylinder head bolts. Eight of them. They were all neatly deposited over the side. Three months passed before I was able to secure replacement parts. Fish swam unmolested in the sea, ducks bobbed about with impunity, and large fir logs eminently suited for the kitchen stove drifted majestically past.

Visitors to the station were fascinated with the crow, delighted to see him perch close at hand and show no fear. Invariably they would ask to have a photograph taken with this feathered ham. Obligingly he would hop onto the offered shoulder. Seconds after the smiling pose was recorded on film, the crow would suddenly clamp his beak on the soft earlobe of his host. He would quickly retreat to a nearby treetop and chuckle heartily.

One year my brother visited the station, and upon his departure was delaying the final goodbyes. Knowing the ferry's sailing time and the condition of the road, I urged him not to be late. He was leaning on the car, twirling the keys around his finger. The crow alit on the car's roof and sidled slowly to the edge, pecking at fir needles and other minor debris as if nothing at all was on his mind. Reading the signals correctly, I warned my brother of the impending raid. Too late! At that very instant the crow seized the keys and flew to the top of the house. But instead of indulging his customary burial-at-sea ritual, he decided to twist the knife and enjoy some quality gloating time on the roof.

Taking a can of dog food, I fetched the extension ladder, climbed to the eavestrough and peered over the edge at my adversary. With his eyeballs blanked out, he was deep into some real belly laughs. It was tough to mouth all those sweet nothings I cajoled him with, all the while tilting the can invitingly to show off its yummy interior.

Just as in the fable of the fox and the crow, greed and vanity prevailed. He dropped the keys, which slid down the roof into my waiting hand, and flapped to my side for an expected reward. I told him what I really thought of him, which felt good, closed the lid and returned the can to the pantry. Finally a last laugh had been reserved for me. Dashing off for the ferry my brother left in a cloud of dust, counselling me as he left to "shoot that damn bird."

We sometimes felt our kids were deprived of many pleasures considered commonplace by the average child. So we ordered from the mail-order catalogue a red vinyl, inflatable, wading pool. Determined not to limit its use due to water shortages I lugged salt water up the cliff, two buckets at a time. It took, as I recall, sixteen pails to fill it. Then I collapsed in the shade to recover. Within minutes the crow arrived for an exploratory bounce on the rim. He circumnavigated the pool two or three times, had a half-hearted bath by fluttering his wings in it, then he retired to think the matter over. I went into the house to find something cool to drink, returning in minutes to find flattened vinyl and a wet lawn. Strategic holes were revealed around the pool's outside perimeter, at ground level. It was a good replication of machine gun fire.

For a number of years I had applied for a highly sought-after lightstation up north. My application was finally accepted. As there were no roads within 40 kilometres of this particular site, I was forced to sell my beloved truck. Driving as hard a bargain as was possible, I managed to sell it to a fellow who boated in to the beach one afternoon. He came back a week later with the agreed-upon $700. Seven crisp, new, hundred-dollar bills. I put them on the kitchen table for safekeeping while we conducted business. We were drawing up the transfer papers on the hood of the truck, when a glimpse of familiar trouble was framed fleetingly in the corner of my eye. The dreaded dark invader had swooped down to the open kitchen window and hopped inside.

Running as fast as I could, I bounded up the stairs three at a time and threw open the door. There in his black bill was the money, all $700 of it. I threw the only thing I had in my hand, a pen, which hit the table with enough clatter to startle him into dropping the load. He beat a hasty retreat through the window and one of the $100 notes fluttered out in his wake. I raced outside and we arrived at the floating currency in a dead heat. A brief tug-of-war ensued in mid-air and the money, minus a beak-shaped bite, was mine.

The new purchaser of the truck was standing nervously by the vehicle. I explained my mad dash; he in turn was fascinated by the bird and insisted on having his picture taken with it. Months later, by mail, he sent me a copy of the photo. There this fellow stood, transfer papers in hand, face contorted in pain, the crow tugging viciously on his ear.

Crowless in my new abode, 480 wonderful kilometres from my tormentor, I received a letter from the replacement keeper. He related some of the villainy he had been forced to endure, and was relieved to report the crow had taken up with a female of his own abominable race. As a result the bird was busy now foraging for food for their young. Stepping out on the porch I filled my pipe and gazed upon the endless expanse of Pacific Ocean and heard the rolling southwest swells breaking ashore. In the moonlight I grew reflective and a picture of a nest high up in a tree appeared, filled with demoniacal spawn, being instructed in the fundamentals of iniquitous behaviour. I was overwhelmed with an urgent desire to send this poor unguarded man a shotgun for Christmas. ◆

East Point lightstation, established in 1888, sits at the southeast corner of Saturna Island, close to the US border. *Photo courtesy Russ Heinl*

AFLAME ON THE WATER

The Final Cruise of the Grappler

DOUGLAS HAMILTON

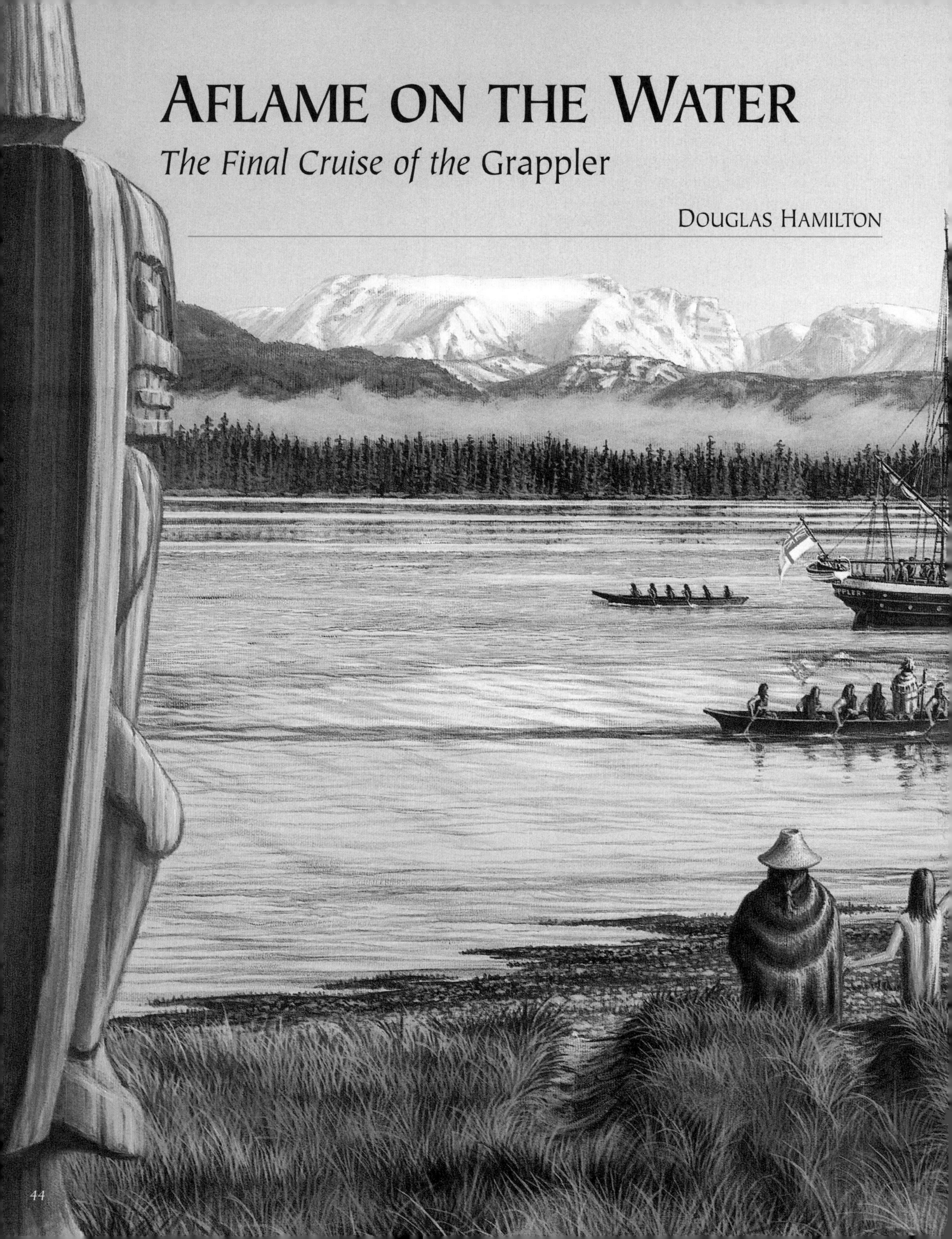

HMS *Grappler* was Britain's muscle on the BC coast during the 1860s, quelling a miners' strike, suppressing Native 'threats' and countering American influence. *Painting by Bill Maximick*

On the night of April 29, 1883, the steamer *Grappler* burned and sank in Seymour Narrows with a loss of over 100 passengers. It was the worst fire aboard ship in British Columbia's maritime history, yet it remains little known.

The tragedy entailed a shameful combination of poor planning, panic and cowardice, but from it arose the beginnings of safety regulations on the West Coast.

The *Grappler* was originally built in 1857 as a Royal Navy gunboat designed to patrol the shallow rivers of the Black Sea during the Crimean War—which was over by the time she was launched. HMS *Grappler* was a handy little steamship—32.3 metres (106 feet) long, 6.1 metres (20 feet) wide, with a draught of only 198 centimetres (6.5 feet). On the cutting edge of the technology of the day, she was powered by a 60 nominal horsepower reciprocating engine (about 240 of today's horsepower), driving a

Stripped of munitions and military livery, the *Grappler* was sold for $2,400 in 1868 and began its career as a coastal freight and passenger carrier. *Photo courtesy BC Museum and Archives*

screw propeller, which pushed her along at a steady 6.5 knots. When the winds were fair, a fore and aft square rig turned her into an adequate sailor. *Grappler* was also well armed, with two of the Royal Navy's most modern breech-loading guns on revolving carriages. Her very name suggested determination and aggression, and several examples of the type were built with similar names including the HMS *Forward*.

With the end of the conflict in the Crimea, Britain looked for a place where the mobility and power of these gunboats could be put to good use. Accordingly, in 1859, *Grappler* and *Forward* were both dispatched to the uncharted coastal waters of British Columbia to counter Indian "threats" and growing American influence in the area. Both gunboats were busy over the next nine years, enforcing law and order, rigorously suppressing any sign of Native rebellion and holding the line against American ambitions in the northwest.

Their most noteworthy moment came during the Lamalcha incident in April 1863. The *Forward* was attempting to apprehend the murderers of three white settlers when it was repulsed with a hail of bullets from the fortified Native village of Lamalcha on Kuper Island. A "boy second class" seaman was killed, and the Royal Navy suffered a major loss of face. Two weeks later both *Grappler* and *Forward* returned to the village and, finding it deserted, burned it to the ground along with several canoes. A large naval force, including the two gunboats, was then quickly assembled to track down the murder suspects hiding on the neighbouring islands. The *Grappler* also served the fledgling coal industry by delivering militia to suppress a bitter, four-month strike against Dunsmuir, Diggle and Company in Nanaimo.

These small warships, crowded and uncomfortable, were not popular with their crews. With the machinery and boilers taking up over half the space between decks, the crew of 36 were squeezed into what remained at the extremities, officers aft, the men forward. Even in an age when seamen had nothing in the way of luxuries afloat, life on these little craft was well below the already low standard.

By 1868, the boilers of both ships were deemed too worn out for repair and they were auctioned off. The *Forward* was sold for $7,000 to agents acting for a Mexican firm. During a period of revolution in that country in the 1870s, she was captured by rebels and burned.

The *Grappler*, being in worse shape, fetched only $2,400. The new owners thought she would be perfect for the rapidly expanding coastal trade. For the next seven years the *Grappler* led a varied career as a freighter jack-of-all-trades, passing through several owners. In late 1875, the steamer was purchased by the famous American, Capt. William Moore, later to be one of the first sourdoughs in the Klondike. Moore proved a better gold digger then shipping tycoon, as the vessel soon became involved in a number of dangerous and unlucky incidents—a portent of the future.

In March of 1876 she went aground on Beacon Rock in Nanaimo Harbour and was beached on the mudflats of the Millstone River for repairs. She was soon aground again, on Sidney Spit near Victoria, causing one shipbuilder to dismiss her as "rotten." However, a steamship inspector disagreed, pronouncing her "sound, staunch, and seaworthy in every respect." Then, in July, while towing the barque *Henry Bruce*, she ran up on D'Arcy Island. The heavy towing rope pulled the *Grappler* over onto her starboard beam, filling her with water, and the old gunboat remained on the rocks for another three weeks.

In November 1880, the ship was hauling a load of heavy machinery from Victoria to Nanaimo when she encountered a fierce southeast gale. The battered hull sprang a leak and she barely made it to Northwest Bay before sinking to her guardrails. Miraculously, the crew was able to patch the hole, and the tug *Pilot* pulled her to safety during a lull in the storm. These repeated groundings undoubtedly played a role in the final tragedy. Although the hull and boiler remained certified, the boiler and firebox were set in brickwork that may have been fatally weakened by this series of mishaps.

In late April 1883, the *Grappler* departed Victoria for points north with a crew of about eight whites and several Native coal carriers. Her captain, John F. Jagers, was experienced, having served as mate and then master of the Hudson's Bay Company *Beaver*. The old gunboat was packed to bursting with lumber, cannery supplies, 50 kegs of blasting powder, 30 white passengers, and more than 100 Chinese cannery workers. On April 29, she docked in Departure Bay to take on 40 tons of coal and unload the blasting powder—a good thing, as it turned out. Anxious to maintain schedule, the ship took on a new pilot and was back on her way by 4 p.m.

At about 10 p.m. during slack tide with a calm sea, the steamer was plodding towards Seymour Narrows and approaching the infamous Ripple Rock, when the mate reported "the smell of fire." Most of the white passengers were sleeping in the few staterooms and temporary berths between decks, while the Chinese had stretched out on the freight wherever they could. Jagers went forward and opened the hatch for inspection.

Steam and sail moor side by side in Nanaimo in the late 1800s. Despite the burgeoning maritime activity on the West Coast, there were no safety standards or inspections—until the catastrophe of the *Grappler*. *Harbour Publishing photo*

"I went below and found a strong smell of fire, but no flame; I went from the after part of the ship along the boiler to the forward part of the ship to the back connection of the boiler. I smelt smoke; I naturally went to look for fire where there was most heat...I went to call the mate, and did not go below after that; I could not get down."

Unfortunately, the brick firebox was inaccessible due to the heavy bulkheads and freight stored below. A large iron plate used for cooking was fitted over the firebox, and it was later surmised that something carelessly stowed had fallen on the plate. But, spontaneous combustion in the coal bunkers or a coal oil lamp may also have been responsible.

Whatever the cause, the fire moved with horrifying speed. Crew members tried ineffectually to haul coal away from the spreading inferno, but were quickly driven topside by the heat and smoke. Capt. Jagers ordered the hatches sealed, sounded five short blasts of the whistle, and set course for nearby Duncan Bay on Vancouver Island. "For God's sake, say nothing about it to the passengers—keep it quiet!" his first mate, John Smith, urged the captain. It was a strange and futile admonition, as the smoke, yelling, and clatter of running feet made it clear to all that something was going very wrong.

Attempts to fight the growing conflagration were seriously hindered by the darkness and lack of available equipment. Only a small lantern in the stern lit the scene; and buckets, hoses and axes were either missing or impossible to locate. James Jones, a passenger, reported:

> The crew were not sufficient; two hands, a mate, and an Indian were all that I saw. There was only one light in the after part of the boat; I did not hear anyone ask for lights until the time of the fire... There was no effort to stop the fire; there was hose, but I saw no water raised. I should judge there were 120 persons between decks; there was a hatchway aft, where it would be easy to escape; I can't say whether any went that way; by the other ways the passengers went over each other's heads. After the fire was discovered, it was about eight minutes until the ship was in flames.

It quickly became apparent that there was a severe shortage of lifejackets and lifeboat space aboard. *Grappler* had originally been equipped with three lifeboats, but the largest had been left in Victoria. Three flat-bottomed fishing skiffs stowed on deck were considered a sufficient replacement. Unfortunately, these ungainly boats were missing oars and oarlocks, and their draining plugs had been removed for the trip north. The remaining two lifeboats had places for only 22. Sixty life preservers were supposedly on board, but few of the survivors reported finding any.

Meanwhile the old gunboat was steaming on full ahead, completely out of control. Her wheel ropes had burned through and the throttle controls were firmly jammed. Chaos reigned as everyone rushed the boats in a panic. Passenger Robert K. Hall described the scene.

> Men, some of them half-dressed running frantically to and fro, half bereft of reason, calling on others to save them, the cries of the horrified Chinamen adding to the fearful confusion... As fast as a boat was lowered men jumped into it—whites, Chinese, Indians—the coolies actually attempting to save their property, throwing clothing and bags of rice into the boats which capsized almost as soon as they were lowered. I could see there was no chance of saving my life by these means and took a set of steps, made it fast to a line, and threw it overboard, allowing it to tow alongside. When I saw the vessel had become completely unmanageable and there was no possibility of running her ashore I dropped overboard, cast off the line and supported by the steps was rapidly borne away with the current.

The crew made little effort to organize an evacuation. David Jones and several panicked passengers attempted to launch boats from the speeding ship with predictable results.

Opposite: Chinese labourers were in great demand in the late 19th century as dockworkers, miners, railway workers and canners, but they were often ill-treated. Racial attitudes and the language barrier added to the chaos when fire swept the *Grappler*. *Photo courtesy Vancouver Maritime Museum*

> We swung the boat out, and started to lower her. They let go very quick at the forward tackle, and we could not clear the rope. The after fall fouled, and the boat hung at an angle, she was ... 8 or 10 [feet above the water]. I said to somebody "cut that fall." After they cut it, the boat turned somersault; I came up and grasped a rope from the ship, and asked to be hauled up; they hauled me a short distance, and let me fall into the water again. I then struck out to swim to shore ...

Henry McCluskey was awakened by his nephew and immediately ran on deck searching for a bucket and hoses. He found no hose and only one bucket, which was half full of fish soaking for the cook. McCluskey lashed two barrels together and was about to go over the side when "... I saw Mr. Steel [the engineer] with one lifebuoy and one life-preserver. I said 'You are pretty well fixed for life-preservers.' I did not ask for one; he said nothing. I saw one life-preserver on the captain; this was after I saw Mr. Steel with two life-preservers; I saw a deck-hand named Conlan with a life-preserver; that makes four, all the life-preservers I saw."

Indeed, Capt. Jagers seemed more concerned with salvaging the ship's strongbox than with passengers.

> I then told the captain it was getting warm and was time to be getting ashore. I saw the safe, at the end of the windlass, close to the captain. I saw something like a stocking with money in the captain's hand. When I said it was time to go, the captain said "I won't go yet."

McCluskey then went looking for an axe to chop down the foremast, which would have floated 15 to 20 persons, but he was forced to retreat before the flames and entered the water with no flotation. He swam partway to shore and came upon several men clinging to a spar.

> Mr. Steel, with his life-preserver on, came up and got on the spar; then a Chinamen came and got on the spar; that made four altogether. I told the men who had life-preservers to get off and let the spar float lighter; they did not get off.

Fortunately, they were soon rescued by Capt. John McAlister, one of the few heroes of this debacle. This experienced sea captain was on his way north to the fishing grounds as a passenger, and it was he who owned the three skiffs stowed on deck. He accompanied Capt. Jagers below, and sizing up the situation, ran back on deck to organize a bucket brigade. When this proved impossible, McAlister raced forward and tipped one of his skiffs into the rushing sea. He jumped in after it, clambered aboard, and was soon followed by a white man and a Chinese. They salvaged a bamboo cane and broom from floating debris and painfully began to paddle their way towards Quadra Island (then called Valdes Island), picking up "five or six men ... and two or three Chinamen," as the Victoria *Daily Colonist* later related.

> Suddenly, without warning, the *Grappler* turned and bore directly down on their fragile craft, passing within a few yards and singeing all with her fiery breath. The steamer kept going backwards and forwards in an erratic manner, the passengers shrieking and yelling for assistance and the flames spreading rapidly over the vessel.

The courageous McAlister ferried his passengers to shore, and immediately set out once again using broken bits of lumber for oars. He pulled aboard "a Chinaman, a Siwash, Steel, the engineer, and several other white men" and returned to shore to build a fire for the survivors. Further rescue attempts soon became impossible as the already desperate situation took a severe turn for the worse. At about 11 p.m., the tide began to ebb.

HMS *Grappler* (foreground) rests at anchor in Vancouver's harbour in the early 1860s, along with two more British warships, *Shearwater* and *Malacca*. *Photo courtesy Vancouver Maritime Museum*

Even today, the tidal rips in Seymour Narrows run at over 15 knots, making it one of the most dangerous stretches of water on the coast. In 1883, Ripple Rock lay in the centre of the channel, creating a boiling maelstrom for the unwary or unlucky. (Ripple Rock was destroyed in 1958 with 1,237 tonnes of explosives.) As the tidal flow strengthened, the struggling survivors were relentlessly sucked into a frigid hell of roaring white rapids that had consumed many a full-sized ship over the years.

David Brown clung to one of McAlister's upturned skiffs and drifted "among some Chinamen who were supporting themselves with various articles. Two or three grabbed my legs and I felt my hold slackening. I exerted all my strength and managed to free myself." However, on sighting an exhausted white man clinging to a plank, Brown helpfully pulled him aboard.

> I had long before this lost sight of the ill-fated *Grappler*, but my companion and I kept our spirits till we heard the roar of rapids and felt the increased strength of the current. We were spun round and round in the whirlpools, sometimes under water and sometimes above, but held on like grim death. At last, about an hour after sunrise we drifted ashore on an island and were found in the afternoon by a couple of Indians in a canoe, who took us to a camp of loggers.

Passenger John Cardano broke his arm trying to launch one of the boats. He described using his remaining fist to punch his way on board one of McAlister's skiffs, occupied by two terrified Chinese. Around midnight the steamer's engine finally stopped and she grounded near Duncan Bay "wrapped in flames from stem to stern." A number of small explosions were heard as the *Grappler* burned through most of the night.

This was clearly one of those terrible disasters in which just about everything that could go wrong did so with a vengeance. So many contributing factors—an irresponsible crew, the darkness of a cold April night, the dearth of lifejackets, buckets, axes, hoses and lifeboat space, the ship barrelling along out of control, the vicious tidal rapids—all combined at the worst possible place and time. The clash of language and culture between the scores of Chinese workers and the 30-odd white passengers and crew then turned a very bad situation into a catastrophe. Most of the Chinese were very recent arrivals with little understanding of the language and customs of the new country. The resulting lack of communication between the two groups made it impossible to stem panic and issue coherent directions for firefighting and a safe evacuation.

British Columbia was wracked by racial tension in the early 1880s. Burgeoning mines, roads and railways required more manpower than the province could furnish, so contractors were forced to import large numbers of workers from China and other Asian countries. It was said that two Chinese miners could do the work of three whites—and do it for less money per worker. The influx reached a peak in 1882 when 8,083 of these Chinese workers arrived in the province, compared to 6,679 white immigrants. An ugly racist backlash developed as whites moved to secure their position in the workplace. The railway work camps in particular seethed with discontent, and less than two weeks after the disaster one Chinese was killed and several critically injured in a violent confrontation at Camp 37 near Lytton.

On the doomed *Grappler*, each race viewed the other as if from another planet—jabbering nonsense, worshipping false gods and looking to steal each other's livelihoods. With all these barriers, co-operation between the two groups was clearly impossible.

At dawn the next day, McAlister made his way to the Kwakwaka'wakw Native village near Cape Mudge for help. Canoes were immediately sent out to scour the beaches, and the survivors were brought back to the village, where they were very well treated before being transferred by steamer to Nanaimo. Twenty-one Caucasians, two Indians and only 13 Chinese survived the sinking. Ten to 12 whites and about 100 Asian passengers perished, but the true number is unknown because there was no official passenger list and many bodies were never recovered. One crew member was lost. At the inquest, even Capt. Jagers seemed to have had little idea as to how many were onboard at the time. "I think I had 100 passengers as near as I can tell, besides those belonging to the ship; I suppose there were about 30 white men and 70 Chinamen . . . " As we have seen, a passenger estimated 120 were between the decks before the fire. More would have been topside.

The hulk of the *Grappler* was found drifting with the tide, her hull burned to the waterline, and "thin as a wafer." She remained afloat for another half hour while Salmon River Natives clambered aboard to salvage what they could. Of particular concern was the ship's safe, which was said to contain at least $1,000. The Natives found and hauled out the strongbox, and $170.50 was salvaged in "half-melted silver coinage." The remainder, no doubt safe in Capt. Jagers' sock, was never recovered. *Grappler* then suddenly flooded and sank, almost taking two Natives along with her. She went down in 30 fathoms, about 1.5 kilometres southeast of Ripple Rock. The next day the receiver of wrecks arrived and thanked the Natives for their kindness and gallant service.

Almost immediately, questions were raised about the safety of the vessel and the competence of its crew. Although most of the victims were Chinese, it was the death of passenger Donald McPhail that prompted a coroner's inquest. After several days of testimony from survivors (no Chinese or Natives were called), the jurors concluded that McPhail had died by drowning caused by the "accidental burning" of the ship. Arthur Vipond, BC's inspector of steamships, noted that the *Grappler* and her boiler had been examined just a few months before and found sound. "I should think the *Grappler*, as to her hull and machinery, at the time I inspected her, was fit to carry passengers, but not as to her equipment."

Capt. Jagers lost credibility when he revealed that his mate's certificate had been confiscated. "I have lost it: not in this country." Under no legal obligation, he declined to tell the jurors when, where or how. Jagers noted that there were few requirements for operating a passenger vessel in British Columbia waters, and that, as captain, he needed neither a mate's licence nor a certificate from the Board of Trade. In fact, ship passenger travel was almost completely unregulated in the province.

The coroner's report, while critical of the captain and crew, was not damning in its findings. No serious laws had been broken, and the steamship line was neither fined nor required to pay compensation. The coroner ruled that the ship was not licensed to carry passengers, and that it had not made sufficient provision for their safety. The owners and officers were found to be "guilty of culpable negligence in allowing said steamer to leave this port in the condition she was, and [we] respectfully call the attention of the Government to the absolute necessity of having a duly authorized Inspector appointed for that purpose."

That was the one positive outcome of this tragedy: The lackadaisical approach to safety at sea, and the absence of regulations and inspections for passenger vessels was no longer acceptable. Marine transportation in rapidly growing British Columbia had become too important to be left to chance. No more catastrophes on this scale would be tolerated. ◆

Source Notes

Arnett, Chris. *The Terror of the Coast*, Talonbooks, Burnaby BC, 1999.
Daily Colonist, Victoria BC, May 4–20, 1883
Gough, Barry M. *Gunboat Frontier, British Maritime Authority and Northwest Coast Indians 1846–1890*, UBC Press, Vancouver: 1984.
Morton, James. *In the Sea of Sterile Mountains, The Chinese in British Columbia*, J.S. Douglas Ltd. Vancouver: 1974.
Paterson, T.W. "*Grappler's* Fateful Voyage," Canadian West Magazine, Number 10, pp. 152–155, Winter 1987.
Pemberton, A.F. *The* Grappler *Disaster, Proceedings Before the Coroner*, May 15, 1883, Pamphlet at Provincial Archives of British Columbia.

MEMORIES OF CEEPEECEE

Life at a West Coast Cannery

ALDER A. BLOOM

It was late August in 1937 when I first sighted Ceepeecee, or should I say when I first smelled it. I was on the *Princess Maquinna*, bound for Zeballos, the gold-mining boom town on the west coast of Vancouver Island, in search of a job. When the boat tied up at the little dock on the north side of Hecate Channel, behind Nootka Island, a few girls and women rushed on board to buy goodies and I went ashore to see the cannery and reduction plant.

The plants were in full operation, the cannery on salmon and the reduction plant on salmon offal and pilchards (sardines). It was very smelly, but so are most industrial towns, each in its own way. To someone looking for work, the smell meant money. Zeballos was 10 miles or so away, so I just took a cursory look, filed it away for future use, and returned to the boat. Little did I know that I would spend four years at this plant and meet the girl I would marry.

When the boat pulled out I was at the rail waving goodbye with the rest of the tourists. We travelled maybe two miles up-coast to McBride Bay and tied up again. At this site a big sawmill was being built and the boat had a lot of freight to unload so I went ashore to have a look around. I found the boss, asked for a job and was hired. They were expecting carpenters on the boat and none had shown up, so I was the lucky one. I spent 10 months at McBride Bay, then worked for the Gibson brothers at their logging camps and for Nootka Packing Company at Nootka, and then at Port Albion before returning to Ceepeecee in the fall of 1941 to work for Delbert Lutes.

Ceepeecee, or CPC, was short for California Packing Corporation, the American company that built the plant in 1926 to process pilchards. In 1934 they sold it to Nelson Brothers Fisheries, who added the salmon cannery. Richard and Norman Nelson had been trolling and packing fish on the West Coast for some years; in 1933, they bought the St. Mungo cannery on the southern shore of the Fraser River near Annieville. After their purchase of Ceepeecee they went on to become one of the major fishing companies in the province.

At Ceepeecee, in addition to the cannery and reduction plant, there was a manager's bungalow with a couple of VIP visiting rooms, a two-storey staff house, a couple dozen houses and apartments

Pages 56–57: Wartime view of Ceepeecee leaves no doubt of the hamlet's purpose. The long, white-sided building with dark roof jutting into the inlet is the cannery and fish house. Beyond are two warehouses and the reduction plant. A freighter is tied up at the end of the dock, while a flotilla of fish boats stretches out beside it. Along the shore are the workers' houses and bunkhouses; the China House, and Native village are to the lower right. Midway up the right side of the photo is a long, dark building with white trim—the company store and office. Above and perpendicular to it, the long, white building is the recreation hall. And the taller white building at the right, half obscured by trees, is the church.

Opposite: For most of its life Ceepeecee was accessible only by water, and this was the first scene to greet all arrivals: A cluster of wood-frame buildings huddled between the forest and the shore at the north end of Tahsis Inlet.

Below: Ceepeecee was founded at the head of Tahsis Inlet, a long and dangerous voyage from Victoria. In the days before factory ships and refrigeration, however, canning had to take place close to the fishery.

for married people, and the bunkhouses and cookhouse. Everything was very Spartan but they did have running water, a sewer running out to the saltchuck and electric lights. Mr. Lee, the Chinese cook, and his helper served tasty and abundant meals for the crew; outsiders could get a meal by buying a voucher at the office.

Del Lutes was the manager and Mac McLean was the plant foreman. Lutes grew up around the canneries in Steveston and, like McLean, was a real coastal character. He had a voice and vocabulary suitable for a muleskinner and I guess he came by it naturally, because he did drive freight wagons from Steveston to Vancouver over a road, cut through the forest, now known as Granville Street. Lutes was everything at Ceepeecee: plant manager, office manager, postmaster, storekeeper, cannery and reduction boss (he had a foreman in each of these plants but they didn't dare make a move without first consulting him), oil agent, shipping agent, and harbourmaster.

He was virtually king over Ceepeecee and the boats that operated out of his plant. The only contacts he had with head office were the *Maquinna*'s bimonthly trips and a radio wireless that transmitted only in Morse code. Lutes and the boat skippers were left to make all the day-to-day decisions on their own.

Small wonder, then, that Lutes became a bit autocratic. He was Mr. Ceepeecee, loved and respected by some, hated by others. His word was law. He got into many scrapes around the town and mines of Zeballos. But he had good fish sense and I think he made money for the company that far outstripped his indiscretions. I ended up working for him for 20 years.

I was the local carpenter and with one or two helpers we took care of all the buildings and plant repairs. Apart from the actual machinery, everything

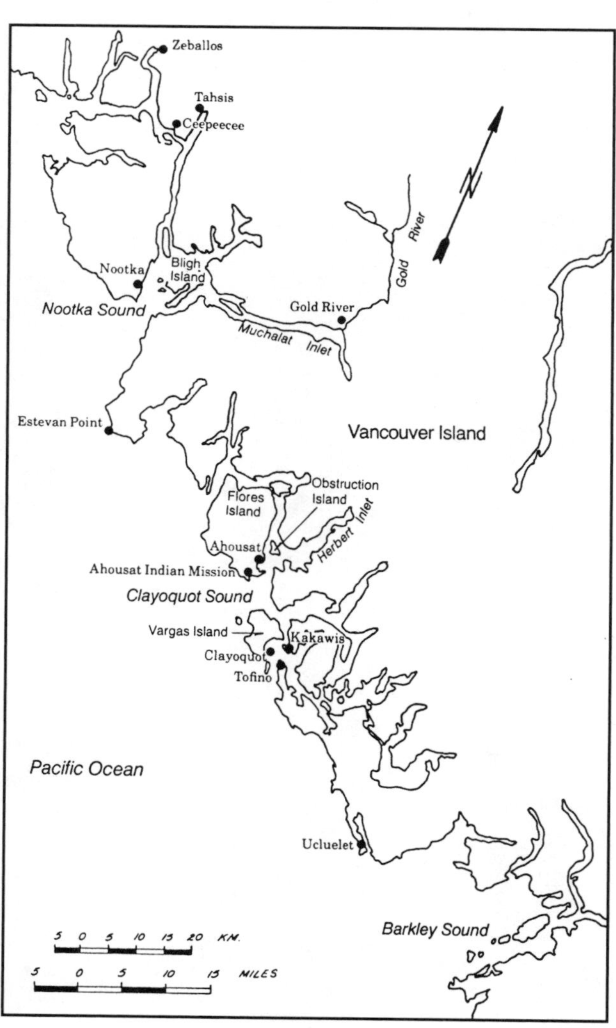

in the cannery was built of wood, so we were kept busy. We built and repaired houses, added onto the store and office, drove piles and repaired docks, built fish bins and flumes, erected a big recreation hall, put in a marine ways—and did boat repairs in our spare time. When the plants were running I often worked alone; when they were slack I often had several helpers as Lutes tried to keep the crews busy.

Neil McLeod, the storekeeper, had at least one of everything one might need. Somehow he could always find the required article in the store or warehouse. And while he was looking, he often found a half-empty bottle of Scotch that he had stashed away and forgotten about, so he was always happy to go on a scrounging spree away from prying eyes.

His assistant was a guy named Joe Hicks. Among other things, he was the butcher. The meat came in bulk—quarters, halves or in boxes—every 10 days and Joe kept it in the store freezer, the only cold storage in the camp. Joe had the job of doling out the meat to the cookhouse, boats, families and others. He had standing orders to take care of the cookhouse and the boats first and the rest of us were to share the remainder, but somehow he managed to keep everybody happy—and all for 25 cents a pound in the early 1940s. With his meat supply and his hearty laugh, Joe was a popular guy. He also had an affinity for the bottled goods and could put away more than his share at a sitting with very little effect.

When I moved to Ceepeecee, Joe was living alone in a company house and I moved in with him. There was a bedroom that Joe used and I had a cot in the living room. My job was strictly from eight to five, except for an emergency, but I soon found out that a storekeeper had no such hours. There were bangs on the door at all hours and Joe would get up to give a boat its grub and supplies.

Women make the most of a sunny spell and a break from cannery work to get a little exercise on Ceepeecee's main street. That's Florence Bloom skipping double dutch.

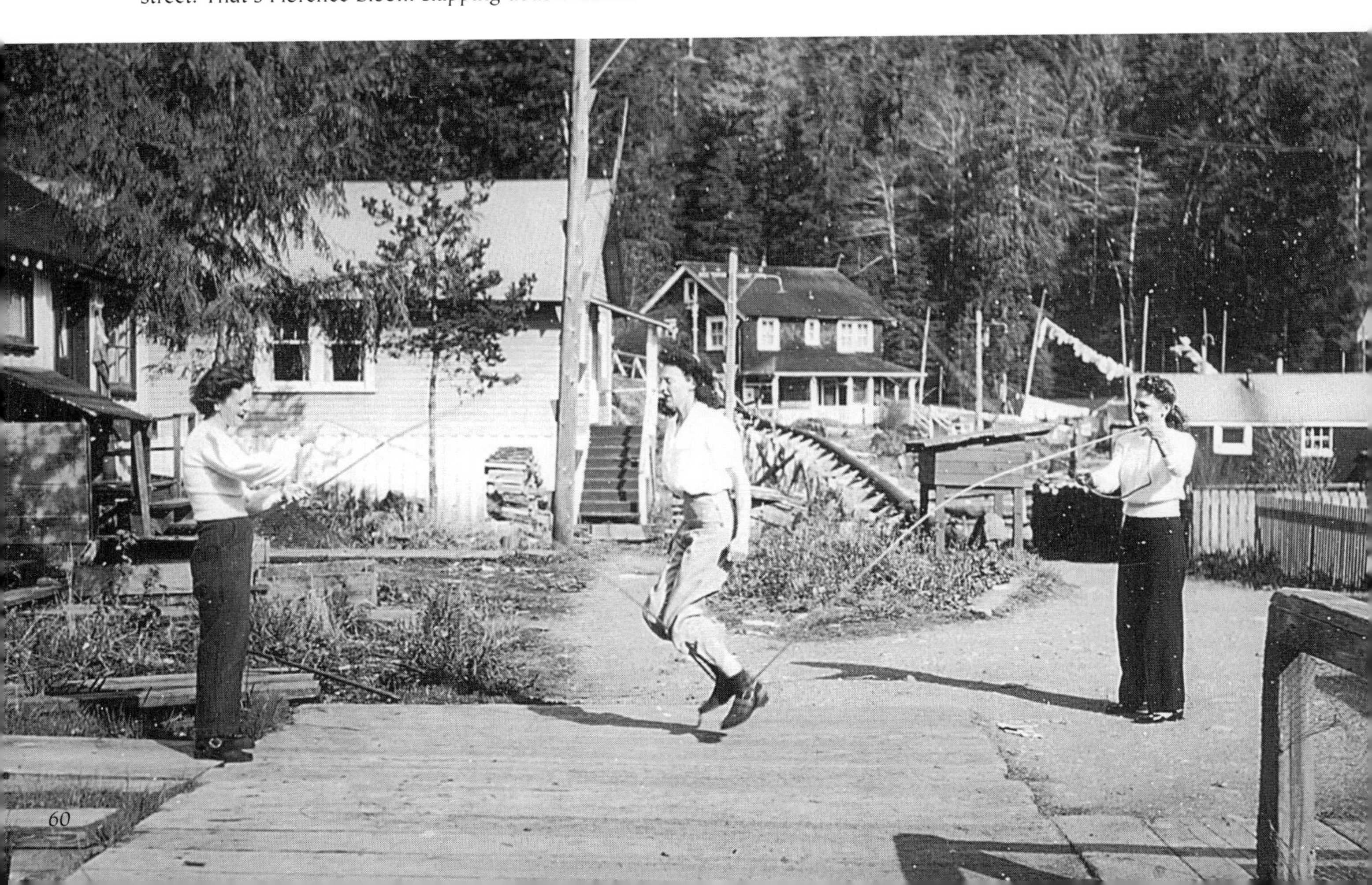

During the pilchard run the plant never stopped. Pilchards are a very oily fish and wouldn't keep for long in a boat. As a packer loaded with pilchards came within sight of the plant, the skipper would blow his whistle to alert the unloaders and they would be waiting to drop the marine leg (a bucket-type conveyer system) into the hold as soon as the boat tied up. The packers often came in with deck loads, barely floating and with the bilge pumps going full blast. The four-man unloading crew started work right away, shovelling the deck load into the hold so the marine leg's buckets could pick up the fish. The marine leg would clamour and groan, powered by a little steam engine, as it dug its way down through the fish. When the fish quit sliding into the buckets the unloaders pulled their hip boots up to their belts, clambered into the hold and plied their big scoop shovels with all their strength, never stopping until the hold was empty. Then they raised the marine leg out of the hold and back on the dock as the fishermen washed down the boat. By then the boat would have its supplies on board, along with any mail or messages, and it would head back to the fishing ground.

Fishermen delivered their catch on a per-ton basis and that's how the unloaders worked, too. They made good money, compared to the plant workers, but few people envied them the job. They were on call night and day and as long as there was room in the plant they were expected to keep working, because the packers had to get back to the grounds as soon as possible.

The head unloader in my day was Oscar Olsen, a medium-sized man but tough as nails. When a packer arrived it was his job to lower the marine leg into the hold and start it operating. When the elevator rested on the bottom of the hold Oscar would climb down and join the other three men shovelling. He also had stomach ulcers and when he started to shovel he invariably became sick and had to empty his stomach over the rail before he could get down to business with the old shovel. But he never complained or failed to do his share. Because of their odd hours the unloaders had their own bunkhouse but Oscar had his wife and his 14-year-old, Ronnie, in camp so he had a company house. They were exceptional neighbours.

The reduction plant crews worked a 12-hour shift, then returned after supper for another two hours piling meal in the warehouse—100-pound (45-kilogram) bags piled 14 high. It was hard work and all for 35 cents an hour, all straight time. An average of 13 people worked each shift. There were five or six skilled positions and these men were paid by the month regardless of the hours worked. They almost always were white men. Natives were assigned some of the more menial jobs, not because they weren't capable of doing better, but they weren't considered dependable enough. The key men all had to be on the job or the plant couldn't operate, as the meal and oil moved from one process to the next continuously until the meal was in the big sacks and the oil was refined and in the tanks ready for shipping.

To refine the fish oil, the press liquid was pumped to tanks and heated by steam coils in the tank. The lighter oils went to the top and the sediment stayed at the bottom. As more liquid was added to the settling tank it filled to the top and the oil spilled down a trough to another tank, and then another, and finally it was refined. Later they developed mechanical separators that were used in the last stages. The sediment in the bottom of the tanks was washed out onto the beach and this had a lot to do with the rotten smell around reduction plants. Later the fish companies were forced to put in expensive evaporator plants to process this sediment and turn it into fish meal. The operator on the oil deck also became permeated with this smell. It steamed right into his pores, and when an oil deckman sweated, he smelled like a codfish. At the end of the season it took many steam baths to remove the smell and even then one never knew for sure.

The fish oil was stored in a number of steel tanks around the plant, most of them on solid ground, but there were a few smaller ones on pilings over the

Left to right: The men's bunkhouse, manager's bungalow, staff house and, at the far right, part of the Native village. Not visible behind the staff house is the China House. The pipe on trestles banking from the centre to the bottom left carries water from a creek behind the town.

beach. One night, the foundations under two of the tanks collapsed and thousands of gallons of refined oil, ready to be shipped, was spilled out on the beach.

For many years the 100-pound burlap fish meal bags were toted to the warehouse on steamer trucks and stood on end, close to but not touching the neighbouring sacks. This allowed the meal to oxidize and cool off. This method took up a lot of space as the bags often had to stand for more than one shift before they were cool enough to move to the warehouse, where they were piled in a solid mass 14 high. But it worked.

During the war years they started using special paper bags; supposedly these could be piled immediately without standing around to cool. It made for big savings in both labour and space, so Lutes adopted the new system. At first it was okay, but then they must have had a batch of oily meal and the bags began burning in the pile. The warehouse was more than half full and it was a terrible thing. Lutes got crews of men to dig down into the pile until they came to the hot spots—always near the bottom—removed the bags that were hot and hoped for the best. In short order there would be smoke from another area and they would dig again. Finally, in desperation, Lutes called in a freighter and shipped out the meal. They were heading for Vancouver but the meal started to burn again and the freighter pulled into Victoria and unloaded the works. Nelson Bros. opened up all the sacks, reground the meal—by this time it was like concrete—and resacked it. The company took a big loss on that deal and Lutes wasn't anybody's fair-haired boy for some time.

The cannery took many more people to operate than the reduction plant. In the early days the reduction plant workers were mostly single white men, but the addition of the cannery required a lot of female help. Counting the machine men, the Chinese men,

Native men and women, Japanese women, and the white girls, I suppose there were 75 or more people in the cannery crew. The machine men, like their counterparts in the reduction plant, were paid by the month regardless of hours worked. The other white men got 35 cents an hour, while Chinese men and women got 25 cents an hour.

During the fall fishing season there were always fish waiting to be canned, usually on scows tied up to the floats with swarms of screaming gulls overhead and on the scows. It was not an appetizing sight. The cannery ran from eight in the morning till 10 at night and then the cleaning crew and maintenance men took over to steam clean and prepare the cannery for another day. As long as there were fish, there were no weekends; every day was the same. People got tired but they didn't mind the long hours. They were just thinking of the paycheque and winter coming on.

All out-of-town canneries, like Ceepeecee, had a bunkhouse for Japanese girls and Ceepeecee was no exception. Japanese men fished for the canneries and Japanese women worked in them, usually washing fish and filling cans. The Japanese women had unfailing good humour and their smiling faces brightened the cannery shed. Their bunkhouse crowded in 15 to 20 girls and a very strict house mother, and every once in awhile a Japanese fisherman would drop in to see how things were going and to read the riot act if required. They kept strictly to themselves when not in the cannery and there it was all work. The only thing that the white folks thought a little strange—and secretly envied—was their hot tubs. These were wooden tubs about six feet in diameter, with walls about four feet high, set up outside, filled with water and heated with wood fires under the tanks. The Japanese stood in these tanks and soaked away their aches and pains. And the elite of today with their spas and their wine glasses think they invented the hot tub!

When war was declared on Japan, the Canadian Japanese were herded to camps in the Interior of BC and in southern Alberta. Their boats and property were confiscated and a bunch of hardworking, capable and frugal Canadians were treated like prisoners of war. They soon became valued residents in their new home territories. The fruit growers had the most knowledgeable workers and pickers they could ever hope for. The canneries suffered the most, other than the Japanese themselves, of course. The white fishermen licked their chops in glee. There had long been enmity between the two factions; now the whites had things their own way as well as the chance to pick up good boats for a song. Also, once more the Indian fisherman had a chance to get back on an equal footing with the white man. They got better boats, but it was still hard for the individual Indian fisherman to get his boat and gear ready to go fishing when the season opened. He was always a few days late whereas the Japanese were ready and waiting days ahead. When the war ended the canners made a concerted effort to get the Japanese back on the coast and into the fish boats where they belonged.

Usually when there was a shortage of cannery women, the Native women took up the slack, but there was an accommodation problem. They lived in the Native village: two long buildings facing each other with a plank walkway between them. They were built on piles over the water to make sanitation easy. The houses were divided into two-room suites. One room had a small wood-burning cook stove, a table and some chairs or benches and a work counter. The garbage went out the door or sometimes through a hole in the floor. The toilets were separate, built over the water. The Indian women never travelled alone but brought their entire family with them, men as well as kids. Often each suite had 10 or more people living in it but only one or two cannery workers. The Native women had to take care of them all, even if they worked long hours in the cannery.

The other main labour force at all canneries were the Chinese men, who were the mainstay of BC canneries from the start. They had finished their labours on the railroad in 1885 and the canneries were a lifesaver for many of them. Very few could speak

English so a bilingual foreman was required and this led to the contractor system, whereby a Chinese businessman would contract to supply most of the cannery labour for so much a case. Each company had its own contractor and the amount paid was usually kept secret.

The company supplied the China House, a two-storey building with a kitchen lean-to. The kitchen always had a big, brick wood-burning stove, built on site, with two or more woks built into the top. All the cooking was done in these woks; rice and tea were their main dishes. The main floor had the office and a room for the foreman and the dining room with its little four-man tables for dining and playing domino gambling games.

The upstairs was a big open ram pasture [men's dormitory], filled with single bunks made from wooden boards and hung with gunny sacks to give a little privacy. The first Chinese worked for $30 or $40 a month, for three or four months, but later it changed to 25 cents an hour. They were willing and able to do most any job that came up, and with a good foreman they could accomplish almost any task.

When Lutes put in a new 12-inch wooden pipeline from the dam to the plant—a distance of about two miles—the job of transporting the wood stave pipe and laying it out along the proposed line fell to the Chinese men. They had to carry it over the rocky creek bed, a horrendous job. They managed it with ropes under the pipe and four men on each side of a 20-foot length of pipe, with the ropes tied to sticks across their shoulders. They would rest in a squatting position and at a signal they would all straighten up, lifting the pipe clear of the rocks, stagger up the creek a few yards and then drop it again for a rest. Eventually they reached their goal and could return downhill for another pipe. It was quite an accomplishment. The wooden supports were cut on the site and the pipes were hammered into place by a couple of out-of-work fishermen. Once more Ceepeecee had a water supply with enough pressure to operate a water wheel for night lights so the diesel generator could be shut down.

During the war years when young male help was hard to get, the companies went after white girls and the more stable married men. To attract them, they offered almost year-round work. To accommodate these couples and the white girls, the company built and moved in more bunkhouses and small houses and somehow managed to house everybody. The single women took care of their own quarters but took their meals in the cookhouse with the men, though at separate tables. Most of the time with married couples, the wife worked in the cannery also. In spite of the low wages, the long hours resulted in a good yearly family income.

Lutes ran a very strict camp but he had to relent a little during the war years. Esperanza Hotel, just 15 minutes away by boat, was a modern building with a good-sized beer parlour, built in 1938 to tap the sawmill trade from McBride Bay. When the sawmill shut down, they found that the loggers, cannery workers and fishermen gave them an adequate business. The town of Zeballos had more to offer with hotels, cafes, shows, bootleggers—and the frontier necessity, a bawdy house. The cannery crews patronized Zeballos very little. It was hard to get to and the cannery hours were prohibitive. We built a big recreation hall to help occupy their time but Lutes' dry laws still sent many of them to the hotel for weekend bashes.

There was a little Scotsman working in the reduction plant and he could squeeze out some very swingy music on his little accordion. He went to the hotel on weekends and the girls spent the night doing their fast jazzy steps with any of the boys who could move that fast. I couldn't so I sat, talked and drank beer whenever I was present, which wasn't very often. They were happy nights and there was no trouble.

One Sunday morning, Scotty didn't check in for his reduction plant shift so a search was started. Scotty travelled in his own little skiff and tied it up at the unloading dock. He had to climb a ladder to get to the dock and somehow he fell. We found him at low tide resting on the bottom below the ladder. Scotty was everybody's friend and he gave more

The young Bloom family—Alder, Florence and son Bob—in Ceepeecee, 1946

pleasure to the crew than anyone in camp. In a place where radio reception was very poor, his little accordion was a godsend. It was sad that he had to go so tragically and alone after having spent hours entertaining an appreciative audience.

Back in the fall of 1940, before I started working at Ceepeecee, I was at the cannery picking up supplies. It was in the fall, when there was a lull before the winter herring started. Most of the crew had gone for holidays but there were maintenance men working and a few of the girls had stayed on to paint machinery. One of them was Florence French, from Vancouver. Florence noticed me going by and gave me a big smile, which I returned. A few minutes later when I was in the Ceepeecee store, she glided in, smiled again, bought her cigarettes and went back to work. I bought my supplies and went back to camp. Once I started working at Ceepeecee, we spent much time together. On October 31, 1942 we were married. We were the first of several Ceepeecee couples to get married; like ours, most of those marriages turned out well. Our son Bob was born in Port Alberni on August 27, 1943.

During the war years I was kept busy with building and repairs. Fishing was seasonal. First we had the salmon from the trollers in the spring, then pilchards for both the cannery and the reduction plant all summer, and herring after Christmas for both plants. It was a year-round deal. Ceepeecee was considered essential to the war effort as the government wanted the canned fish, especially the herring put up in oval cans with tomato sauce.

The only indications of a war at Ceepeecee were the blackout curtains, the absence of the neat and smiling Japanese girls to brighten up the drab cannery and camp, and, a little later, the food rationing. However, the store had such good quotas that we hardly noticed the rationing. Radio reception was very poor so we weren't bombarded with war news and we only received mail once every 10 days. The Air Force had a listening post at the mouth of Esperanza Inlet—at Ferrer Point, I think it was—so we had an occasional Canadian airman as a visitor.

The fishermen's navy was our only real protector. The government took 40 of the biggest and best packers and seine boats from the fishing companies to make up this force and the ex-fishermen and skippers had the time of their lives patrolling the coast. I'll bet that, had the coast been invaded, they would have put up a good fight and gone down with their ships.

With our big recreation hall and the arrival of the white girls Ceepeecee became a regular call for the Navy. They enjoyed our dances and I have to admit that they were a credit to the Navy and behaved in an orderly fashion.

One day, an Army man arrived to alert us about the Japanese incendiary balloons that were being sent over on the prevailing winds to try to set BC forests on fire. It sounded very farfetched to us, but apparently they took the threat very seriously, as they did the shelling of Estevan Point, a mere 20 or 30 miles south of us. At any rate this fellow organized a Ranger unit and each man joining up was given a 30-30 rifle and shells.

There were always accidents that kept Mrs. Davies, the Ceepeecee nurse, busy: hands jammed in gibbing [fish-head-removing] machines, cuts, bruises and burns, hands pierced by fish bones and infected. One time the cannery lineman's leg was burned by steam and he went around on crutches for a long time. Another poor fellow stepped in a screw conveyor and lost a foot. A Chinese man sat down to rest and didn't get up again. The Chinese were very superstitious and they refused to touch the fellow. The cannery maintenance people had to seal him in an airtight container for shipment south on the *Maquinna*.

There was a doctor at Zeballos, but that was two hours from Ceepeecee by boat. Dr. McLean, the mission doctor, was only half an hour away and he did some exceptional things in emergencies but he always maintained that he would rather save souls than bodies, so most people were reluctant to visit him if they had an alternative. Jack McKay was one fellow who had no alternative. He developed terrible stomach pains and lay in his bunk for a number of days with no relief. We had a couple of guys in camp with ulcers who lived on baking soda; Lutes insisted that Jack was in the same category and left him in Mrs. Davies' care. Ritchie Nelson paid us a visit, took one look and ordered Jack taken to the Mission Hospital. Dr. McLean operated that night under the most primitive of conditions, with people holding lamps and flashlights, and removed a badly infected duodenal ulcer and undoubtedly saved his life. That was one of the fantastic things that McLean did, but he often messed up smaller things.

McLean travelled around the camps in his far-from-safe little boat, often overloaded with his people, giving sing-songs and preaching in good old evangelical style. He eventually built a church at Ceepeecee and held regular services.

In the early '40s the pilchards became scarce and then disappeared completely. Everyone—the plants, the fishermen and the crews—were geared up for a big year and then there was nothing. The fishermen staggered about the ocean like chickens with their heads cut off, not willing to believe that millions of tons of fish could just disappear. Some of them rigged up poles and tried to catch some tuna that showed up in coastal waters. That wasn't enough to keep the ambitious fishermen happy so they turned to the salmon. Before long their efficient fishing machines took a toll on the salmon also.

With the pilchards gone the fishermen were in a quandary, but the shore worker was left destitute. They expected a four-month session of 12-hour days so their 35 cents an hour would grow into a winter's stake. Instead they were given a few hours of work now and then to pay for their board and tobacco. The salmon cannery still operated but the plants depending on the pilchards, including Ceepeecee, were very dismal places. The crews had no money to pay their way out. Some managed to work their way out on the *Maquinna*, but the rest just had to sit back and wait.

Ceepeecee struggled on for a bit, but was shut down for good in 1951. Fish boats using refrigeration or freezers could stay out longer and deliver their fish right to the cities. New regulations were imposed and government inspectors took a dim view of the old, wooden canneries. Up and down the coast, companies found it too expensive to renovate the out-of-town canneries so they abandoned them. Some were torn down, some were sold, but the others were just left to rot. Nelson Bros. built a reduction plant at Steveston and got big, fast packers and barges to haul the fish. Other companies also built modern canneries in the major cities. Over the years, the canning industry was consolidated and now a few companies control the whole industry.

Most of the buildings at Ceepeecee were destroyed by fire in 1954. Only the little boat ways remains. ◆

We are sad to report that while we were compiling this issue of Raincoast Chronicles, *author Alder A. Bloom passed away at his home in Vancouver. Mr. Bloom spent 40 years in the fishing industry, starting in 1938. He worked at Ceepeecee from 1940 to 1946, then went on to work at all the Nelson Bros. plants and camps in BC. Mr. Bloom was very familiar with the BC coast, its history and many of its most notable characters. He spent the years after his retirement from BC Packers documenting the colourful history he lived through. He has left the people of BC a rich legacy in his writing.*

THE CANNING LINE

A Working Salmon Cannery in Photos

In addition to his lucid writing about Ceepeecee, Alder Bloom left behind this remarkable photographic record of Ceepeecee's cannery, documenting the processing of salmon from fish floor to warehouse.

1. With only a few boxes and planks holding back a sea of salmon on the cannery floor (later the fish would be stored in bins) three men work a Smith Butchering Machine, dubbed the iron chink, in the early 20th century because it replaced 30 Chinese men on the butchering table. The man on the right wields a long-handled, one-tined fork called a pew (or pugh), skewering fish and heaving them up to the table beside the machine. The fellow on the far left sorts the fish and places them head-first on a conveyor, which takes them past a knife that removes the heads. The man in the middle then feeds the butchering machine, which has a large spiked wheel that grips the back of the fish and holds it while knives remove the fins and open the belly. Brushes and water gut and clean the fish. The head, tail, fins and offal drop through a hole in the floor to a flume that floats them to the reduction plant, while the roughly cleaned fish is deposited on a belt that leads to the washers. There are electric lights, but everything else is powered by a steam engine, so that shafts, countershafts, belts and pulleys clank and shimmy from one end of the cannery to the other. It looks messy, but the whole place is cleaned with live steam and hot water at the end of each shift.

2. From the iron chink, a belt takes the fish to the washing line, 10 or more young women assigned to individual work stations. A door opens as required to deliver more fish to the worker's trough, filled with running water. She thoroughly cleans, scrapes and washes the fish, then puts it in the bin behind her, which is monitored for both quality control and worker productivity. These girls are on their feet for 12 hours or more a day, for 25 cents an hour, all straight time. Even so, they fare better than their predecessors, Japanese girls who were paid on a piecework basis—so much per bin—before they were rounded up and sent to internment camps. According to author Alder Bloom, it was always a sore spot with the canners that it took so many girls to wash the fish, but they were never able to devise a different way to do it, even in the modern-day canneries.

3. This machine, one of the first modern cannery machines, cuts the salmon into pieces sized to fit either a one-pound or half-pound can. The circular knives on top are very sharp and can be spaced as required; the worker here is operating the left-hand side, set up for half-pound cans. The blades on the right side are spaced farther apart, for one-pound cans. Rectangular buckets, with slats aligned with the knives, are bolted to a continuous chain that loops around sprockets at the top and bottom of the machine. As the bucket comes up from the bottom a worker throws a fish into it, and as it goes over the top the rotating blades pass through the slats, slicing the salmon. The resulting pieces of fish are collected in a hopper, loaded onto a push cart and taken to the canning line.

4. (page 70) On the canning line, cut-up fish are loaded into galvanized buckets perched at an angle in front of the fillers. Each worker takes half-pound cans from a basket behind her, fills them with fish and puts them in the trays on the middle shelf in front of her. This is piecework: When the tray is full a tally man patrolling the filler stations will remove it and punch her card. Only the half-pound tins are filled by hand; most fish are loaded by machine into one-pound cans.

5. (page 71) Workers empty trays of full cans onto the conveyor chain that takes them to the steam box. Salt is added before the lid is loosely fastened. Other women across from these workers are the patchers, who remove from the line any can that looks light, weigh it, add fish if required and return it to the line. Patching is a specialized job that goes to more senior workers. They get the same pay, but a bit more respect from both the women on the line and from management.

4

6

7

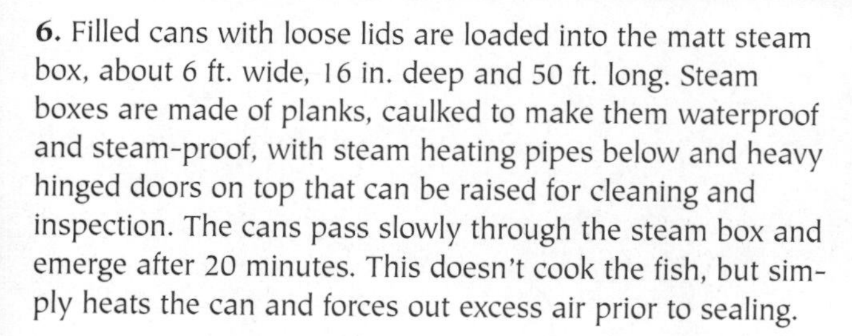

6. Filled cans with loose lids are loaded into the matt steam box, about 6 ft. wide, 16 in. deep and 50 ft. long. Steam boxes are made of planks, caulked to make them waterproof and steam-proof, with steam heating pipes below and heavy hinged doors on top that can be raised for cleaning and inspection. The cans pass slowly through the steam box and emerge after 20 minutes. This doesn't cook the fish, but simply heats the can and forces out excess air prior to sealing.

7. Cans slowly emerge from the discharge end of the steam box and slide down a metal guideway to a conveyor that will take them to the crimping machine, where the lids are sealed tight.

8. Half-pound tins are sealed as they come off the filling line. From here they are loaded onto buggies and shunted into the retorts for cooking. If this machine and others on the half-pound line look small for such a large operation, it's because 60 years ago only the choicest fish were sold in half-pound cans. These were mainly coho; West Coast troller operators of this era did not fish for sockeye, believing they could not be caught with hooks in the open sea. Other fish were sold in one-pound cans, and the cannery has two long packing lines dedicated to the larger size.

9. A woman operates a machine filling one-pound cans. She feeds a cleaned, whole fish into the machine, which uses a series of plungers to push the fish into open cans descending from the can loft, (right). These are used in the fall for the big dog salmon (chum) run. Note the wooden shield protecting the operator's head from oil from the shaft bearing.

10. A mechanic and his helper adjust a filling machine as it runs, while filled cans are conveyed to the patchers (next photo). The women in the background are operating a second filling machine.

11. Native women work on the patching line from the filling machine. During the fall 10,000 or more cases of chum are canned at Ceepeecee, and every tin in every case must pass these women. They remove light cans from the line, add the correct amount of fish and return the tins to the line. From here the cans move through a salter and then to the closing machine.

12. The closing machine loosely crimps the lids on the cans before they enter the vacuum machine.

13. The vacuum machine at the end of a tall-can line sucks the air out of the cans and seals them airtight. This method replaced the steam box.

12
13
48 - 1'S TALLS
48 - 1'S TALLS

14

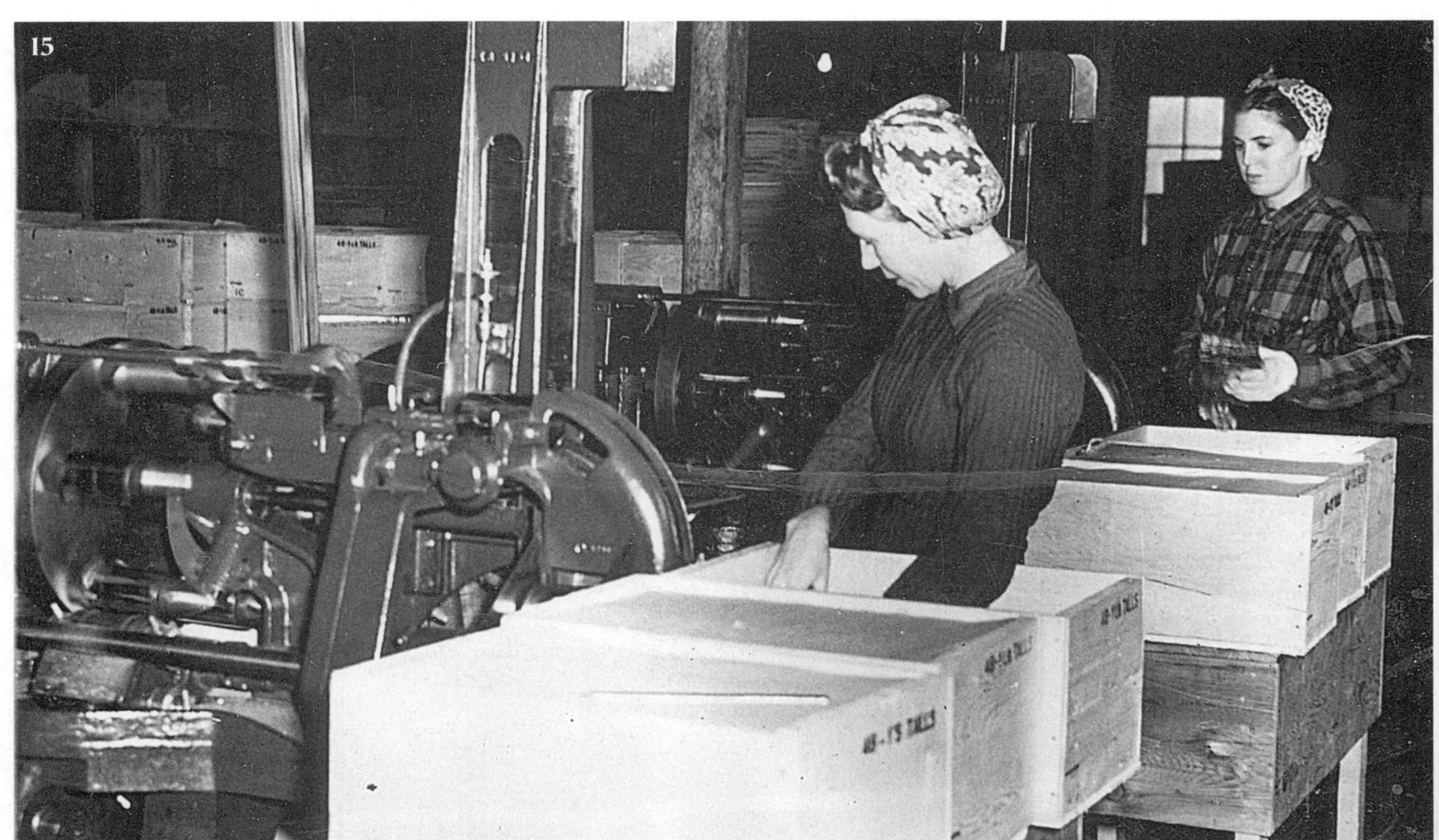
15

14. Both vacuum machines working full-tilt at the end of either one-pound line.

15. Cans are shipped to Ceepeecee in pieces—one box containing the sides, packed as flattened cylinders, another box containing the round ends. These women are loading the flattened sides into a machine that restores their cylindrical shape.

16. In the can loft, the machines in the foreground receive the re-formed cylinders from the machines to the left and rear of the picture, attach one end to each can, then pass it to the canning line below. These machines are leased from the can supplier.

17. The man to the right is either raising or lowering the door to one of Ceepeecee's five or six cannery retorts, or steam cookers. Visible in the retort is a dolly loaded with seven trays of sealed tall cans; behind it are four more loaded dollies. The door is locked in place before the steam is turned on, and the canned fish is cooked for 70 minutes or so.

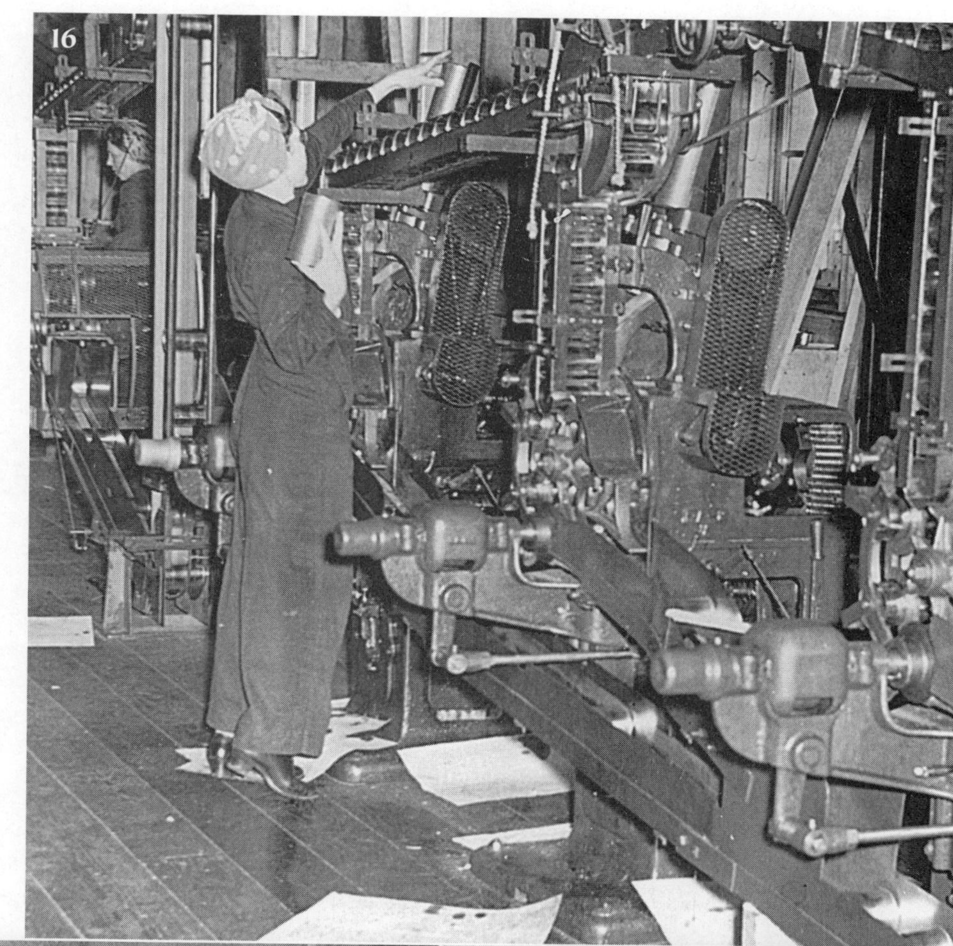
16

17

18

19

18. Using a long hook that grips the axle, men pull a hot dolly out of the retort, then push it to the box-up warehouse where the cans are left to cool. As their temperature drops, the vacuum in the cans pulls in the ends with a sharp ping. Protruding lids signal a faulty seal; packers will set such cans aside for recanning or disposal.

19. Filling crates is murder on the back, but the box-up warehouse is clean, dry and warm, so the job usually goes to older women with seniority.

20. Chinese box makers nail the tops on full boxes of canned salmon. They are paid an hourly rate for this, but the assembly of the crates in the box loft is piecework, and the men work long hours to make a good wage. In the 1950s cardboard cartons will replace the wooden boxes.

21. Before the advent of forklifts, boxes are shunted to the warehouse by steamer truck and piled by hand. It's no easy job, as each box weighs about 50 lb.

Salt, Salmon and Psalms

Wes Huson and the Growth of Alert Bay

Pat Wastell Norris

Sometimes, before I was old enough to go to school, I spent days with my grandparents in Alert Bay. In the afternoons, after my grandmother had scrubbed clothes, cooked a lot of wonderful food on a wood stove, washed and trimmed the oil lamps and done her bookkeeping (for she was the family's financial officer), she changed into a fresh pair of lisle stockings, put on a navy "afternoon dress," did up her hair and we went out. I took her hand and together we walked along the wide gravel path that followed the shoreline. Our route led us right through a Kwakwaka'wakw Indian village. On one side of the path was a row of longhouses fronted by towering totem poles so that we walked beneath the cruel, proud gaze of thunderbirds and passed bears exhibiting ferocious teeth. We developed a nodding acquaintance with huge naked figures with pursed lips, extended arms and sightless eyes that stared out to sea. On the opposite side of the path were dugout canoes pulled up on the pebbly beach and, in season, big beach fires ringed with intricate racks of drying salmon. On these excursions we met barefoot children clutching tiny kittens with crusted eyes and dodged half-starved dogs scratching and nipping at their limitless supplies of fleas. Neither my grandmother nor I found anything noteworthy in these surroundings. She had lived in Alert Bay since 1909 and I had never known anything else.

Alert Bay offered other, more unsettling, experiences for a small girl from a virtually teetotal household. If our boat was tied to one of the docks in "downtown" Alert Bay on a Friday or Saturday afternoon, and if I accompanied my father up the street on an errand, I had to edge around the drunks who lay sprawled on the side of the road mumbling and shouting (fortunately unintelligible) curses.

Left: Oblivious to the charms of scenery or tribal art, boys hang out on the waterfront sometime during the 1920s, throwing stones and gnerally looking for mischief. *Photo courtesy Pat Wastell Norris*

Opposite: A towering totem, emblem of Alert Bay's Kwakwaka'wakw culture, alongside one of the clapboard structures that began to replace traditional bighouses. *Photo courtesy Pat Wastell Norris*

Inevitably their faces were covered with blood—the result of a difference of opinion with their fellows.

"The Bay is a terrible place," said my mother.

What it was, of course, was a rip-roaring fishing village. Before Charlie Pepper built the Rainbow Theatre, he showed movies every Saturday night in Alert Bay's Anglican Church Hall. More often than not they were shoot-'em-up "cowboys and Indians" films which were, in the days before political correctness set in, extremely popular with the audience. The real Indians yelled encouragement to the phony Indians on the screen. And small boys, sitting on wooden benches in the front row, totally caught up in the action on the screen, stared up in wonderment. When the story line got particularly exciting, they shrieked and pummelled each other until the bench fell over, throwing them all on the floor.

The audience gave little thought to the fact that they were watching Hollywood's version of the Wild West while right outside the door of the hall the real Wild West was going full tilt. Outside was a rickety little village that included, not the Last Chance Saloon, but the Nimpkish Hotel. The steeds weren't tied to hitching posts outside the bank but were moored five deep at the string of docks lining the shore. And since it was Saturday night in fishing season and everyone had just been paid, the good guys and the bad guys were locked in combat—rolling around on the gravel road that formed the main drag. Fueled by alcohol and testosterone, they flailed away, barely noticed by the passersby.

It started out quite differently. It started, you could say, in 1792.

At 10 p.m. on July 19 of that year, Captain George Vancouver's ship *Discovery* arrived at the mouth of what is now the Nimpkish River and anchored just outside a stretch of sand and sedge grass that formed a small island. At that latitude, at that time of year and at that hour there was just enough light left for the crew to distinguish the mouth of the river and, across the strait, the long mound of an island. And there was just enough light for the native inhabitants

of the village at the river's mouth to witness the arrival of the *Discovery*.

As impressive as the ship's appearance must have been to people who travelled by canoe, it probably wasn't the first time they had seen a sailing ship, for in the last quarter of the 18th century Spanish, British and French explorers had all found their way to the coast of what was to become British Columbia. In unwieldy sailing ships the explorers fumbled their way through the coast's narrow channels, ferocious tides and rock-choked passages, its reefs and its fog. They navigated without the aid of GPS, the sweeping line of radar or the flashing numbers of a depth sounder. They didn't even have a chart for, in time, the unwieldy ships' purpose was to survey this coast and *produce* charts.

These foreign explorers substituted seamanship and local knowledge for technology. For this wasn't a totally empty wilderness, however much it might have appeared to be. Scattered bands of Natives lived in villages lost in the vast jigsaw puzzle of land and sea, kept at the water's edge by immense trees and a jungle of undergrowth. Their sustenance came from the sea, so they were skilled seamen, wise in the ways of this treacherous coast and its complicated tides. Consulted by officers of various majesties' ships, the Natives gave advice, warned of hazards and shared knowledge hard won by a people who had paddled their canoes here for thousands of years.

It was another 50 years before the ships of the Royal Navy began to map the area. For 13 years HMS *Alert* and HMS *Cormorant* and later the steam-powered HMS *Plumper* undertook a detailed survey of British Columbia's coastal waters. By 1860 Johnstone and Broughton Straits, Queen Charlotte Sound, Knight Inlet "and adjacent channels" had been surveyed and mapped in the London offices of the British Hydrographic Service. For three shillings the Royal Navy produced a chart that could be used with confidence today. The village at the mouth of the Nimpkish River was identified as Cheslakee, after its chief, and the sandy islet became Flagstaff Island. The island across the strait was named after HMS *Cormorant* and the curve of bay after HMS *Alert*.

And then, some 10 years after the island and its bay were identified on charts, Westly Alden Huson stepped ashore in Alert Bay. An early resident of Alert Bay, now long gone, remembers hearing that years before, "Wes" Huson had arrived on a sailing sloop, possibly one of many owned by traders plying the coast with goods to sell to the Native people. Huson, an American from New York state, had come to the West Coast convinced he would find a fortune in gold and other minerals.

Huson, the only white man in this village of 400 Native Indian people, promptly set out to explore the surrounding country. Almost immediately he had a brush with success. At Fort Rupert he was told of a coal deposit at Suquash, just north of the Nimpkish River. He obtained a lease for the property from the Crown and worked hard to develop "The North Pacific Coal Company." And he nearly succeeded; he came within a hair's breadth of becoming a coal baron. If it hadn't been for Robert Dunsmuir, who found better quality coal much nearer the markets, Wes Huson might have been the one to build himself a castle in Victoria. Instead he went back to his search for another mineral bonanza. Periodically he boarded the SS *Beaver* and travelled to Victoria with samples of copper and iron ore, marble and granite.

In 1874, the first cannery was established on the lower Fraser River and canned, salted and pickled salmon was produced and exported for the first time. Perhaps, Huson thought, there was an opportunity offered by this new industry. He and his friend and partner Stephen Spencer pooled their slender resources and built a primitive little saltery on the waterfront at Alert Bay where there was deepwater mooring for steamships and easy access to the huge salmon runs in the nearby Nimpkish River.

As a location, Alert Bay had an incomparable advantage. Not only were the Nimpkish River salmon plentiful, they were superior to the salmon caught elsewhere. The Japanese, discriminating

Salmon from Wes Huson's cannery made its way to market under a variety of brand names.

consumers from the very beginning, had discovered that salmon from the Nimpkish River and from Simoom Sound had a firm texture ideal for salting. So, by 1878 a Mr. Fujiyama and a Mr. Sukiyama, knowledgeable in the customer's preferences, were in charge of Spencer and Huson's saltery. Before long steamships were calling to take the five-foot wooden boxes of fish to Vancouver and then to Japan.

Early on the enterprise ran into an unexpected problem, however. There was a modest market and a bountiful supply of fish but not enough people to process them. In this sparsely populated wilderness the only available labourers were the peripatetic Natives who moved back and forth to the Cheslakee village—much farther afield if there was a wedding or potlatch to attend. The paper *Kwakwaka'wakw Settlements 1775–1920* states: "There is conflicting evidence about when the inhabitants of Whulk (the native name for the Cheslakee village, meaning bluff) crossed to Alert Bay. Part of the problem is that Whulk continued to be a fishing site after it was abandoned as a winter village." Whether they lived at Whulk or at Alert Bay, which was also a seasonal village, persuading these inhabitants to come to work in the saltery on a regular basis was more difficult than Huson and company had expected. They found themselves introducing a radical idea—"working for a living"—to a people for whom the concept was entirely foreign. The First Nations people worked only enough to exist on a subsistence level; their days, then, weren't workdays as such but days in which work, play, art, music and celebration all blended seamlessly into a whole. Untouched by the Puritan work ethic, the men found nothing shameful about spending whole days talking or gambling or simply sitting in the sun and doing nothing at all. So these people paddled across to Alert Bay and turned up at the saltery out of curiosity or when the spirit moved them, but the concept of a regular workday had no appeal at all.

It took a combination of religion and materialism to solve the problem. First Wes Huson persuaded the Reverend Alfred Hall, who had established a mission at Fort Rupert, to move to Alert Bay, noting that Alert Bay was more central in relation to the surrounding villages than Fort Rupert. Huson also promised to supply the mission with land and to build a mission house. Thus persuaded, the Reverend and Mrs. Hall moved to Alert Bay the same year that the saltery was established.

The second lure came in the form of material goods. There was a store in Alert Bay; periodically a steamer called with supplies and goods of all kinds which could be bought with wages. This proved an irresistible attraction. Alert Bay might owe its name to the survey ship HMS *Alert* but it owes its existence to people like Wes Huson and his partner Stephen Spencer. Capitalism had arrived and the Native way of life was changed forever.

By the late 1800s, a footpath followed the pebble beach that curved along Cormorant Island's wide bay, stretching a mile or two from the mission house and the little sawmill at one end to John Robilliard's log house at the other. In between lay the Kwakwaka'wakw village marked by a row of massive longhouses that stood shoulder to shoulder, their great flat facades facing the sea. Their distinctive shallow-pitched roof line proclaimed their heritage as did the totem poles that towered in front of them, the fierce faces of wolves, bears and thunderbirds glaring down at passersby. Their only break with tradition was the milled siding that covered their log frames in place of long split cedar shakes. Here and there a Native inhabitant of the village had opted for the more "modern" style of a conventional frame building and here and there the gigantic log frame of a longhouse under construction raised its bulk. For this was a community still taking shape.

Lying in front of the longhouses or pulled up on the beach below were high-prowed dugout canoes. And all along the waterfront was a raised wooden platform built out over the beach. This was the Native equivalent of the Englishman's club and its philosophy was "carpe diem." This was where the men indulged their passion for gambling games and carried on interminable conversations.

The beach itself was the domain of the grandmothers. As they did on the beach at the mouth off the Nimpkish River, the women built big fires that burned continuously in the months when the salmon were running. The fires were encircled by an intricate network of saplings and filleted fish and, as at Cheslakee, a gaggle of barefoot boys kept them supplied with driftwood.

Establishing this village within a village caused some difficulty. The Crown, blithely assuming ownership of the whole coast, had given Wes Huson a lease for the whole of

Cormorant Island. Now some of this land had to be extracted from the lease agreement and designated as a reserve for the people who had lived there first.

A spacious mission house was sited on a portion of this reserve land and when it was completed the Halls left the wilds of Fort Rupert for the dubious charms of Alert Bay. They arrived in a bleak little settlement that could dispirit the cheeriest of souls. The incessant rain bleached the sea, the beach, the piles of driftwood, the handful of frame buildings and the row of longhouses to a weathered grey. Even the dark trees were greyed with mist. And then the impenetrable darkness of a wilderness night obliterated it all, except for windows glowing from kerosene lamps or a bobbing lantern carried by someone walking along the waterfront.

Kwakwaka'wakw fishermen soon became a vital part of the new industry. Paddling across the strait to the mouth of the Nimpkish, they trolled the tides from their dugout canoes and delivered their catch to the saltery where Native women cleaned, salted and packed it. By 1881, only three years after its establishment, the saltery's owners became convinced that canned salmon was the product of the future. So they bought some early canning equipment and converted the saltery to a cannery. The little mission sawmill, originally intended to teach skills and supply the community with lumber, became a bona fide box factory and the man-and-wife trollers were soon catching the first Nimpkish River salmon to be put in tins. In Victoria, Stephen Spencer did his best to sell this new product. He was not particularly successful.

In 1901, the Right Reverend W.W. Perrin, bishop of the diocese of BC, visited Alert Bay as part of his clerical duties. This man was one of an astounding group of clergy that fanned out across the world promoting the religion of Victorian England, an era that was prim, narrow-minded and utterly convinced of its superiority. Eager to minister to "the heathen," the Right Reverend disembarked from one of the Union steamships and plunged into a busy round of activities.

He was distressed, he noted later, by Kwakwaka'wakw marital arrangements. "The whole question of their marriage customs is full of difficulties. A girl is sold at a very young age to her husband but as soon as she has paid back the purchase money, she is free to leave her husband without disgrace and to be married to another who may be willing to give a larger price for her. In this way a young woman of twenty-one may have lived with four different men and the result is disastrous." (From today's vantage point this arrangement may seem an enlightened response to the problems of monogamy but to a Victorian Englishman it certainly did not.)

Left: Bighouses crowd the waterfront at Alert Bay. The European concept of 'work' as a daily routine with fixed hours was alien to the Kwakwaka'wakw whose everyday life combined fishing, cultural and leisure activities in whatever mixture seemed appropriate. Seeing that money did not motivate his workforce, Huson set up a mission in town to spread Christianity—and with it, the Puritan work ethic.

Above: A dog naps during a quiet afternoon on the waterfront—a contrast to the rip-roaring celebrations when the fishing fleet comes in.

Spectacular totems are juxtaposed with laundry lines along Alert Bay's boardwalk, circa 1912.
Photo courtesy Pat Wastell Norris

On the other hand, the Right Reverend Perrin was considerably buoyed by his visit to the school: "The school children are quite equal to any white children in secular knowledge," he said. "And I only wish that other school children in Canada and England had an equal knowledge of their Bibles."

He was concerned, as many after him were, about the liquor problem. But all in all, he thought, it had been an encouraging visit. He commended Reverend and Mrs. Hall for their devoted service and reboarded the steamship on its return trip to Vancouver.

Wes Huson was still struggling to keep his fledgling business afloat. The government official who had approved his lease for the Suquash coal property noted that Huson and his partners "possessed little means." Lack of capital was certainly one of Huson's problems; another was lack of business contacts. But perhaps his biggest obstacle was his predilection for prospecting. Stephen Spencer was having great difficulty interesting people in Victoria in canned salmon and it seemed to a discouraged Huson that canning fish was nothing more than a sideline that distracted him from the possibilities that prospecting offered. So in 1884, three years after the saltery became a cannery, Wes Huson sold his lease on the 600 acres of property on Cormorant Island that he had obtained in 1870 and left the business for good. Stephen Spencer and his new partner, Thomas Earl, bought out the lease for $1,000. In Earle, Stephen Spencer had found what was needed: a partner who had capital, business experience and invaluable contacts in London.

In 1873 Wes Huson had married Mary Ekegat, a Tlingit woman originally from Alaska. He and his wife were to have 10 children, but in the 19th century a child's chance of reaching adulthood was far from assured. In infancy and early childhood, five of the Huson children succumbed to illness. In 1892 Mary died, too. She was only 44. After her death, the older Huson sons scattered, picking up work where they could find it—in the Yukon and on the Skeena River; crewing on ocean-going steamships and logging on Swanson Island. They always kept in touch with their father, always kept their eyes open for prospecting opportunities and occasionally helped him with his ventures. A younger brother, Spencer, named for his father's friend and former partner, made his contribution by becoming a first-rate hunter. He kept the family supplied with deer, ducks and geese and sold the excess.

As with most householders of the time, theirs was a hand-to-mouth existence. But Wes Huson remained the eternal optimist. Until blindness made it impossible, he continued to file mineral claims and collect ore samples, convinced that one of them would prove to be the motherlode.

In the census of 1881 Wes Huson's profession was listed as "trader" but when he died on December 19, 1912, the Record of Burials listed his profession as "canner" which was perhaps more appropriate. For although Wes Huson never did grasp the fortune that seemed so attainable in his youth, the little saltery that he established with his partner Stephen Spencer changed the lives of the inhabitants of Alert Bay forever. ◆

Although his first love was prospecting, Wes Huson's entrepreneurial skills created a stable economy for Alert Bay. *Photo courtesy BCARS*

Source Notes

Akrigg, G.P.V. and Helen. *BC Place Names*. University of BC, 1997.

Chart (copy) Johnstone & Broughton Straits and Queen Charlotte Sound with Knight Inlet and Adjacent Channels. Admiralty, 1867 (Courtesy B. McClung).

Galois, Robert Michael. *Kwakwaka'wakw Settlements 1775–1920*. Joint publication of University of BC Press and University of Washington Press, 1994.

Gregson, Harry. *A History of Victoria 1842–1970*. The Victoria Observer Publishing co., 1970.

Huson, David. Family correspondence and documents in A.M. Wastell, ms, Provincial Archives, Victoria.

Marshall, James Stirrat. *Adventures in Two Hemispheres: Captain Vancouver's Voyage*. Telex Printing Service, Vancouver, 1955.

Newell, Dianne and Roberts, Arthur. "B.C. Canning Industry," article from *Western Fisheries* Vol. 110 No. 3. University Projects document, March 1984.

Perrin, R.R. Article in *The Church Missionary Intelligencer*. Anglican Church Publication, London 1901.

Vancouver, George. *The Voyage of George Vancouver 1791–1795*. The Hakluyt Society, London, 1984.

A Story in the Snow

Bus Griffiths

You know, when you are in the woods in the wintertime, there are lots of stories to be seen in the snow, if you are observant.

I remember one winter we'd been shut down for snow. On this particular day, I'd just gone out to the woodshed for an armload of wood when the boss's pickup swung into the yard. He climbed out of the truck and I wondered what he had on his mind.

He said, "Buster, you know that series of rock bluffs just past the S-curve in the logging road? Did you ever hunt over them bluffs?"

I said, "Yeah! I've got the odd buck in there. Quite a few does seem to hang around in that area."

The boss laughed. "I'm not interested in the deer," he said. "What's the ground like, and how's the timber?"

I said, "Well, actually it's pretty flat. The rock shows in lots of places, but it's not bad. There's quite a few trees in there. Along the front there's mostly them peewee firs, but when you get in a ways there's some nice stuff."

The boss seemed excited. "Look, I'll pick you up in the morning and run you down to camp. You can take the GMC truck and go up them bluffs. I want you to cruise that timber to see if it would make a worthwhile Cat show. I'll see you in the morning."

With that, he took off.

I was up early the next morning, because I knew the Old Man would expect me to be up in the bush by the regular starting time. Margaret and I had finished breakfast when I saw the lights of the pickup as it swung into the yard, so I grabbed my rigging and headed out.

When I was warming up the GMC truck in camp, the Old Man came to me and said, "I want you to really look over that area and see just how much timber we can get with the Cat. You know the elevation isn't too high and there shouldn't be too much snow. It might make a bit of a winter show for some of you boys. I may be up later."

There was a little snow on the road as I neared the rock bluff area. I pulled into a turnout and parked the truck. I grabbed my axe, and I figured I'd take my lunch bucket. That way I wouldn't have to come back to the truck at lunchtime.

There was about three inches of snow on the ground. I worked my way through, studying and estimating the timber and also the ground. I noticed some old deer tracks and, later in the morning, old tracks of a big cougar. There were lots of signs of squirrels and also marten tracks.

I began to feel the pangs of hunger, so I thought I'd better check the time. I shoved my hand down the waistband of my Bannockburn pants and pulled out my old turnip. Sure enough, chow time. I slipped the strap of my lunch kit off my shoulder, then cut some bark off the dry side of a fir snag, including a large piece for a dry seat. I soon had a nice little fire going, so I cut a forked stick from a blueberry bush for toasting my sandwiches.

I'd barely got seated and had just started to open my lunch bucket when two whisky-jacks came sailing in and plunked in the snow, one on each side of me: A couple of volunteers to help me eat my lunch.

It has always amazed me that these birds are so tame. Even the young birds, that have never seen

I'd barely got seated and had just started to open my lunch bucket when two whisky-jacks came sailing in and plunked in the snow, one on each side of me: A couple of volunteers to help me eat my lunch.

people before, seem devoid of fear and will come down and take food from your hand.

I broke a piece off a sandwich and held it out for one of the birds. It took the piece of bread and flew away. I turned just in time to see the other bird taking off with one of my sandwiches clutched in its feet. When it was about to land in a tree it transferred the sandwich to its bill.

When the whisky-jacks collected their booty they would fly up and tuck it in any handy crotch, where a limb came out from the trunk of the tree.

Close by, and being very secretive, was a Steller's jay. It was watching this performance with great interest. Finally, while the whisky-jacks were down collecting more loot, this wily bird was up pilfering their caches. One of the whisky-jacks, returning to the treetops with more booty, caught the blue thief taking off with its ill-gotten prize. A great squawking match started between the two birds, and they were joined by the other whisky-jack. Shortly, two more whisky-jacks appeared on the scene and the blue jay was lucky to escape with just a few ruffled feathers.

But it was time to get back to work, so I put out my lunch fire and went back to scaling timber and studying the country.

Around mid-afternoon the Old Man showed up. By that time I had a pretty good idea of the lay of the land and the amount of timber available. When I told him what I'd come up with he said, "That's great! There's more than enough wood to keep several of you boys busy until the snow goes and we're ready to start loggin' up on the mountain. I think in the morning you better start blazing out the Cat roads.

I said, "Okay, and I'll mark them out so the fallers can herringbone the timber to the roads, as much as possible."

The next morning there was a little fresh snow, and there's nothing that makes the woods look prettier than a fresh fall of snow.

As I worked back through the timber, marking out the first Cat road, I saw a few fresh deer tracks. These were joined farther along by the tracks of a cougar. Later I saw where the cat had sprang at a deer, but hadn't made a kill.

I was amazed, later in the day, to see the tracks of a fair-sized bear. I thought all bears should be asleep by now. Generally, when a bear doesn't hibernate, it's because it's hungry.

I thought I'd better study the tracks; maybe this fella was hurt. After following the bear's tracks for about a hundred yards, I discovered two things. The bear was injured in the hind quarters—you could see by the tracks that it was dragging the right hind foot. Also, the bear was definitely following the cougar, probably hoping the cat would make a kill, and he'd invite himself to a meal. Sort of an uninvited guest.

The thought struck me that maybe I'd better leave the area and blaze a road in another part of the bluff.

The next morning there was a skiff of fresh snow, and I was blazing a Cat road through a stand of big, scattered fir. I could feel a cold breeze blowing on the back of my neck as I worked through the timber.

Suddenly I came into an open area in time to see the back end of a big bear disappearing into the trees on the far side of the opening. In the snow were the sad remains of a two-point buck deer, and there in front of me was the "story in the snow."

You could see the marks where the cougar had made the kill. The bear must have been quite close and downwind. The cat had started to feed when the bear charged, but there was no sign that the cougar had put up any fight—almost as if it thought, "I'm outta here!"

When a cougar makes a kill, it's what you might call a "tidy diner." It eats what it wants, and if there's snow on the ground, it covers the remains with snow. If there's no snow, the cat will cover the remains with leaves and brush.

On the other hand, a bear is anything but a "tidy diner." This bear had already dragged the carcass of the deer away from the spot where the cougar had made the kill, and before it was through the remains would be spread over quite an area.

I thought I'd better leave and blaze a Cat road into another spot, and let nature take its course.

In the next few days I finished laying out the Cat roads. When I got into the spot where the cougar had made the kill, I could see that the bear had cleaned things up, but had scattered the remains over quite an area.

Nowhere could I see any fresh sign of either animal.

A short time later the fallers moved in and started dropping the timber. I questioned several of them about the animals, but none of them had seen any fresh sign of either the bear or the cougar.

Over the years I've often thought about my "story in the snow," and what a great painting it would make. I could have the cougar lying on the deer, snarling and with a paw up in defensive position, and show the bear rushing in. If I gave the painting a title, it could be along the lines of "Whose Meat?", "Disputed Possession" or "The Uninvited Guest."

However, so far all I've done is think about the painting. Oh well, maybe one of these days . . . ? ◆

The cat had started to feed when the bear charged, but there was no sign that the cougar had put up any fight—almost as if it thought, 'I'm outta here!'

BUS Griffiths
'99

The Tugboat Annie Method

Howard White

I never came across a truer saying than the one about a boat being a hole in the water into which you throw money. I often wondered what kind of person thought it up. It seemed like it should have been someone I knew.

It isn't the idea of the money going in that strikes me quite so much, since most of my boats have been on the do-it-yourself side, as much as the idea of the hole, a temporary disarrangement of the natural order, an offence to oceanic pride on which it

Illustration by Nick Murphy

concentrates its vast resources day and night, trying to set it right. There is only one final aim secretly harboured by any boat, and that is to relinquish its unnatural void by going to the bottom with as much inconvenience as possible to its owner. Some boats will wait whole lifetimes for the chance. I was reminded of this on a New Year's day a few years back.

Our family had this old jointly owned diesel cabin cruiser, the *Pywackett*. It was old enough that its previous history was pretty much lost in the mists of time, but there was a theory it had been built some time in the 1930s in the "foredeck cruiser" style that was popular back then. These boats had great high flush-deck hulls extending back three-quarter way to the stern, where they were punctuated by a skimpy wheelhouse and a small open cockpit. Some do-it-yourselfer had gone at it in the meantime and hacked off most of the foredeck, replacing it with a squarish wheelhouse and after cabin that owed more to carpentry than boatbuilding. (Carpenters think in straight lines; boatbuilders don't.)

Like most pleasure boats, the *Pywackett* lay idle at the dock month in and month out. I knew just by its look it was getting in the mood to sink, but I redoubled my determination to head it off by checking it every day as I drove by. I watched it like an eagle, egged on by my all-too-vivid vision of carpet soaked with crankcase oil and electrical equipment oozing turquoise mush. I began to flatter myself with the notion that perhaps I had reached the stage of grizzled experience where it was no longer possible for a boat to get the best of me. I had to leave it at New Year's for two days, but my sister and her family were holidaying in the cabin beside the dock and Alan and Sharie Farrell, who had lived on boats all their lives, were anchored beside it. They were all watching it especially closely because of the bad weather. I explained to them how you could tell how full the bilge was by watching the waterline at the bow. The bow always settled first.

It made it through the night, apparently floating as normally as it had for fifty years. Both parties of watchers particularly noticed this as late as 10 a.m. But at 10:30 my sister looked out and there it was, its life mission fulfilled, the two-inch high combing around the cockpit the only part of the hull still above water.

I don't get seasick from sailing on boats, but the way sufferers describe it gives a good indication of the sensation I had standing on firm ground taking in that sad sight. I have a job that doesn't give me much time off and I treasure the brief respite of the Christmas–New Year's break. I make the most of it and spin it out as long as I can. Now it was going to be cut short. Worse, my precious downtime was going to be supplanted by a particularly ugly and frantic species of labour.

The usual drill when a boat goes under involves a lot of panicky around-the-clock work as you inch the hulk up the beach over a series of tides. You get logs or empty oil drums alongside and run lines under the hull so the floats are taking as much weight as possible. At the top of the tide you drag the arrangement as close to shore as you can before it hangs up. As the tide falls and the boat grounds, you take up slack on the ropes. When the tide comes in again, the logs lift the hulk higher, and you bump further up the beach. By the second or third tide, if you're lucky, you have the boat sitting up on dry ground. But there's a lot that can go wrong.

When you get the boat up far enough that it starts to come out of the water on a falling tide, if it has a deep-keeled hull like the *Pywackett*'s, it will naturally try to fall over on its side. Not only will this risk smashing the brim-full vessel on the rocks like a water balloon, it means that the rising tide will just flood in over the low side and you won't get it refloated. Like as not it will become one of those disgraced old hulks that adorn the beaches of so many coastal harbours, to the chagrin of the beautification advocates and the delight of Sunday painters.

To avoid this fate you have to get around the side and just at the crucial moment when it begins to heel over, jam a bunch of sturdy timbers in with one end against the rub rail and the other in the mud. Usually the balance point comes when the water around the stern is still over a tall man's head, and I have never discovered a way of navigating through this phase without spending a lot of time underwater. Being made of nice buoyant cedar, the timbers don't really want to keep their heads in the mud. They'd rather tease you by popping up just when you think you've finally arranged the physics of the situation so there's enough lean on the boat to hold them down. The first couple always go in fairly well, but when you get to the last one, you have to rock the boat back up a little to set it in place, but when you do this you take the pressure off the others, and up they pop. It never gets done without at least half a dozen trials, and hysterical cursing only helps so much.

In hypothermic January temperatures and having long since out-matured the wetsuit bought in svelter times, I wasn't looking forward to this part. Nor was I looking forward to the part that comes immediately after, when the tide exposes the hull and fifty tons of trapped water comes to bear on a structure that is designed to hold it out, not in. The stress can break a boat's back, or at least spring the fastenings. You have to go crazy bailing and pumping trying to lower the level of the water inside at the same speed the tide is going down outside, and it's amazing how fast that tide can vacate the premises once it makes up its mind. At this stage the boat is still teetering back and forth, threatening to eject its props, and oily floorboards are floating around inside denying good foothold to frantic bailers. Wet and cold is one thing, but wet and cold and greasy has it beat by a nautical mile.

All of this familiar activity was streaming through my mind as I stared in disgust at the old *Pywackett* that New Year's morning. The gorge rose in my throat, pushed partly by anger and partly by the remains of some stuff I'd put down it the night before. Way too much stuff, as Premier Campbell might say. It was one of those moments, far too frequent in my life, when you get thinking a nice clean lightning strike between the eyeballs might not be such a bad thing.

It was an ugly prospect, but there was no use sulking about it. Your only chance of surviving stuff like that in your right mind is to get up a big head of steam and bull through it, and that is what I resolved to do. Almost.

In my desperation, I began to entertain a goofy idea aimed at avoiding most of the foregoing scenario. It was based on my observation that at this point the old girl had not quite gone under. It was trying desperately, but in those days the family dock was still floating pretty high, and the tie-up ropes on the boat were pretty skookum. They had come tight in just the right way, and were holding the ship just high enough that there was about a half an inch of deck combing still staying dry around the stern.

There's an old story I read years ago in the *Saturday Evening Post* when I was a kid, and it always comes back to me at times like this. It was based on my favourite fictional character, Tugboat Annie, who was the only person in the whole world of mainstream culture who had the faintest shred of plausibility in the eyes of a kid growing up in a logging camp like I was. Most stories you read featured people riding around on underground trains or going up 200-foot-high buildings in things called elevators, and it made for good fun but you couldn't take it seriously. But Tugboat Annie—here was somebody who did something real.

On this occasion she was, as usual, trying to outsmart her arch rival, old Capt. Bullwinkle. Something big had sunk, a barge or a steamship or some such, and the first one who could figure out a way to get it refloated was going to have a big pay day. More important, they were going to have the pleasure of seeing their rival be really, really pissed. Bullwinkle, being better capitalized, had the jump on all the conventional remedies as usual, and Annie's only chance was to employ her superior wits. As usual.

She got on the blower to Seattle's biggest sporting goods supply and ordered three truckloads of ping pong balls. Of course everybody figured the strain had finally got to her, and she had to unleash

Howard White, his son Silas and friend John Skapski (left) prepare for a voyage aboard the Pywackett in happier, pre-submersion days. *White family photo*

a couple of her patented body slams to quell a mutiny. But the ping pong balls showed up just in time, she hooked a big air hose to the sunken barge and with the aid of her on-board air compressor blew those ping-pong balls down into that sunken barge until their collective buoyancy made it pop to the surface. Boy, was that Bullwinkle cheesed...

I didn't have a million ping pong balls handy, but I took inspiration from Annie's example and started toying with the idea that maybe there was some tricky newfangled way of taking advantage of that half-inch of freeboard to make that boat come back up on its own, without going through the three-day hell of dragging it up the rock-bound beach.

I knew it didn't have a big hole in the bottom or anything. The reason it sank could only have been that it took on enough rain to lower that heavy bow down well below the normal water line. The old fir planking on this particular hull had long ago been treated to the "final solution"—a jacket of watertight fibreglass, which stopped sea water from even thinking about leaking in through the bottom. The only trouble was that the fibreglass ended just a few inches above the normal waterline. Above that you were back to the original fir planking chinked between the seams with cotton caulking, which had been allowed to dry out and become about as watertight as the average fishnet. Once the water level came up to that area, swoosh, down she went.

Realizing this, I also realized I only had to think of some cagey Tugboat Annie way of raising her back up to where the dry planking was out of the water, and I could walk away happy. The diesel motor would be fine after this brief a dunking, if you rinsed it with fresh water and changed the oil, and got it running. The rest of the cleanup could wait till the holidays were well past and I was back to being miserable full-time anyway.

I knew where I could rent a couple of high-volume barge pumps capable of sucking the boat dry in short order, if only I could stop new water from washing in through the un-glassed part of the hull, which was so porous the dock's resident herring school was probably swimming through it. I tried to imagine Annie slowing down the incoming water by stiffening it with five tons of Jell-O. Naw, you'd need something stiffer than that to clog these holes . . .

Then it came to me. Poly. Get a nice new 100-foot roll of three-mil poly from the lumberyard and make an envelope of it around the boat. But how to hold it against the sides tightly enough to form a seal against the inrushing water? Maybe, just maybe, when you got the barge pumps going full blast, the tiny current of the water being sucked in through the seams would be enough to draw the poly in against the hull and plug it up.

Well, I know for sure it's not from living right, but that day the Gods were in an uncharacteristic forgiving mood and they smiled on me. The barge pump-and-poly ploy worked so slick I spent about a nanosecond wondering how you could go about filing for a patent on something like that. I just pushed the plastic down around the hull with an oar—being careful not to cause a half-inch ripple that might finally swamp the old girl and send her the rest of the way to the bottom—pulled it tight and fastened it with roofing nails. Then I cranked up the big pumps.

You could almost hear that poly snap as it clamped up against the sides. It wasn't five minutes before the gunwales started to rise, and inside of an hour I had the *Pywackett* sitting up on top of the water like a seagull. I still spent most of my New Year's ripping out oily carpet and roasting salt-soaked electrical gear alongside the turkey, but it sure wasn't as bad as it could have been.

I did manage to save the starter, a nice bonus since those diesel starters cost a bundle, and the little Nissan motor was so tight the water hadn't even got inside it. But the house wiring, which had been cranky enough to start with, never worked again without sparking and smoking. When we got it all scrubbed down, the boat wasn't much funkier than it had always been, but we never really used it again. Once a boat has been underwater you can't relax on it. Eventually we sold it to an oyster farmer on Nelson Island for $1,000, and he rebuilt it into a beautiful yacht, but it sank on him too, and he gave it up for good. You can see her barnacled old hulk today adorning the beach of Blind Bay.

Still, I always keep a boat. Living on the coast without a boat is like living in the Swiss Alps without a pair of skis, in Los Angeles without a car, or in Merritt without a 4X4. You can't quite feel you belong. People come to visit, and what do they think? You're not in tune with your surroundings, not receiving what your place has to offer. If I went to visit someone living in a Wyoming cowtown, I would expect to find a horse. I would expect people there to say that riding through the pine scrub on horseback was in their blood, and that was why they would never live anywhere else. I would expect to feel the pull of this way of life coming through them, pulling at me. Living here in a coastal fishing town, I feel the same way about having a boat, even if the only time I go on it is to bail it and charge the batteries. ◆